6/19/21

THE
KINDNESS
FORMULA

Caring + Character = Success

Make every day a "BIG DAY"!

By Jim Olayos

REGENT PRESS

Berkeley, California

The Kindness Formula
Caring + Character = Success

Copyright © 2020 by Jim Olayos

Published by Regent Press, Berkeley, California

Printed in the United States of America by
DavCo Advertising, Inc., Kinzers, Pennsylvania 17535.

For information, address Jim Olayos
Future Stars Children's Foundation
21 Captains Watch, Shelton, CT 06484
jolayos@sbcglobal.net

Book Design by Anita W. Gunn

ISBN 13: 978-1-58790-538-4
ISBN 10: 1-58790-538-8

Cover Photo: Rob Kinmonth for USA Weekend

Table of Contents

Jimmy Olayos Jr.

2/22/1988-6/8/2019

*"There are some who bring a light so great to the world
that even after they are gone the light remains"*

Dedication

This book is dedicated to the memory of my son, Jimmy Olayos Jr. As a little boy, he was my best friend, my constant companion and my biggest fan. I was proud to be his Dad. As he grew, Jimmy's kind nature developed. His smile was all it took for people to know he cared. He was a great husband to the love of his life Chelsea, and in their time together he constantly found ways to show her how much she meant to him. He was an equally great friend, a loving brother and a role model for so many. His work ethic was beyond compare and I always bragged about Jimmy being the hardest working person I ever met.

Jimmy did more in 31 years than people have done in a lifetime. Jimmy passed away suddenly on June 8, 2019, while competing in a triathlon. In his life, he took on challenges and conquered events like tough mudders, marathons, bike races, road races and even surfing. At Jimmy's funeral, I learned so many more things about him. He was a beloved co-worker who started each day by greeting everyone with "Going to be a BIG DAY" or "Let's have a day!" His infectious smile lit up the room and everyone was uplifted by his positive and optimistic way of living. Jimmy was a true leader at work; he cared about the individual person and did everything possible to make them great physical therapists and better people. All who worked with him were treated like a member of his family.

His loss to all those who loved him has left an empty space in the world and gives me a longing to see that big smile in heaven someday. In the meantime, my hope is to honor him with this book and by making each day a "BIG DAY"!

To make a donation to The Jimmy Olayos Jr. Charitable Trust go to www.BigDayJO.com

Acknowledgments

Over 40 years ago, I began a process of collecting information, jotting down my thoughts and attempting to document certain events of my life. I would then take these items and place them into a large folder for safekeeping. This was done with the hope someday my children would look at the folder's contents, learn a little bit more about me and find a road map for their lives.

About 10 years ago, at the suggestion of my wife Kim, I decided to use the contents of the file to write a book. When asked why I wanted to write the book my answer was in narrow terms, "simply to leave a legacy for my children and their children". As I sit here now I realize this "story" involves many who have touched my life and I take this opportunity to thank them.

To all my students, players and Future Stars campers I thank you for all I have learned from you and for giving me the opportunity to be a part of your lives.

Thanks to my collaborator Brian who helped me organize my thoughts, share his writing skills and act as a sounding board for advice.

Thank you to Bruce Mowday and Simsun Greco whose compassionate hearts, mentorship and wisdom helped me get to the finish line.

A special thanks to Jayne Pillemer, the daughter of one of my best friends, Bill Carapezzi, whose love, guidance and expertise helped me turn my thoughts into a book.

My other best friends, Ron Carapezzi, Jim Whiting, Gene Cellini and the late Tom Clark who never failed my family and me in our greatest times of need.

To my many cousins, my Uncle John, Aunt Susan, Uncle Ray, Uncle Mickey, Aunt Julie, Aunt Shirley, Uncle Andy, Auntie YoYo and her husband Andy who continued that bond and sense of family my mother and father brought into our lives.

To my grandparents Jenny and James Olayos, Nick and Susan Giampaolo who formed the foundation of kindness and love in our family.

To my sister Sueanne Lisi and her husband George and my nephews George, Nick, Jon, and my sister Amy thank you for all your love and support.

To my parents, no words could adequately express my gratitude for your love and sacrifice. My hope is this book becomes a fitting testimonial to your lives.

Finally, to my wife Kim and my four boys, Jimmy (1988-2019), Casey, Brett and Shea you are the reason I wrote this book and the inspiration for everything I have ever done in my life. You have always made me proud and your constant love and support for me is all I ever needed. You are the book, my heart and my life. Thank you and I love you all!

Jim's 60th birthday celebration in Disney with the family

Foreword
Living a Life with Kindness

I was born into a family where love and commitment to each other prevailed. For me, it all started with my mother. My grandmother was diagnosed with terminal cancer when my mother was a teenager, and at the time, there was no hospice, so she was cared for by her family in their home. My grandfather, an electrician, was tasked with the responsibility of providing for and caring for his sick wife and their 4 children. Much of the household responsibilities fell on my mother, the oldest of the four. On a Memorial Day weekend, my grandfather went to work and accidentally touched a live wire. He was electrocuted. My grandmother passed not long after that, leaving my mother to assume the responsibility of raising her two younger sisters, Julie and Susan and her younger brother, John.

By the time I was born, my house was full of family: my parents, my older sister, and my mother's two youngest siblings, who were attending college at the time. I remember very clearly watching my parents selflessly supporting our blended family, emotionally and financially, with my mother as everyone's nurturer. As I grew, I would learn of the continued sacrifices my mother made to do this: forgoing college so that her siblings could go, giving up a job in the insurance world to raise kids. She kept everyone's spirit alive in the wake of the loss of her parents. Every Sunday our house was full of relatives and friends of her brother and sisters and our family. My mother would cook for them all, and my sister and I, the youngest of the family, were given attention from all the visitors. It was here I first felt the value of an open house and an open heart. At my young age, I was unaware of the value of anything material but was constantly shown the benefits of being kind and giving to others.

I also had a great friend and mentor in her brother, my uncle. He took me with him to the various Boys and Girls clubs he worked, let me ride in the club van and allowed me to be the batboy for his

Senior City League baseball team. I watched his interactions with the club kids and the care and concern he showed for each. In turn, they brightened every time they saw him. I knew it and they knew it: my uncle was someone who wanted to help them in their lives. While my mother created a safe and loving life within the home, my uncle showed me the power of giving love to those outside the family. He became a role model and had a powerful influence on me as I was finding myself and who I wanted to be. His example still continues to frame my thoughts, words and the work I do today.

Early on, thanks to my father's and uncle's influences, I fell in love with sports. I also loved to entertain my cousins and friends by making games out of any handy items, which led to my nickname, "Milton Bradley," around the neighborhood. I frequently placed two snack tables at each end of the living room to make goals, and using ping-pong paddles and any ball I could find, we would play our version of hockey. I liked to turn my mother's kitchen stools upside down to form makeshift basketball hoops and again, using any ball we could find, would play basketball. We broke many of my mother's favorite things, as well as wearing her rug out, but we never heard her complain.

As I outgrew the makeshift games, I continued to use sports as a way to organize the neighborhood kids into little friendly competitions. My nature, as learned from my upbringing, was to be inclusive. While those who couldn't play well were otherwise shunned, I made sure everyone was in the game. It didn't matter if you were skilled or not, boy or girl--there was a place for you in our games. I was able to see the joy everyone got in playing and how getting everyone "in the game" allowed them to improve and find things they enjoyed doing. I also viewed how being open and kind to all opened the door to some great friendships that have lasted a lifetime. I realize now this is where I first began my thoughts of a career working with children and how encouraging wholesome outlets could lead to many benefits beyond the game itself.

During my high school years, I played basketball and baseball and ran track. However, during my senior year, a torn ligament in my foot kept me from my dream of playing college basketball. In retrospect, my senior year in high school was a very empty time for me, as I became distanced from sports and the intrinsic values and benefits they provided me throughout my life. I went on to Fairfield University and majored in economics, figuring the education would serve me in business or law. I ultimately chose law with hopes of saving wayward juveniles. I hoped to use my background and influence to help young people in trouble. I hoped I could assist them in finding their value and in turning their lives around. I had an instinctive hope for all that drove me. My mother would say, "You like to water dead flowers." She saw much of herself in me.

During my law school years, I strongly felt I was missing that old connection to kids and sports that I loved so much. My uncle suggested I interview for the position of freshman basketball coach at Masuk High School in Monroe, CT. I got the position and was in my element. Although difficult at times, I was able to juggle my law school workload with coaching high school basketball. I bonded quickly with my players and was fulfilled in seeing my influence on these young players. It triggered my desire to continue coaching and lead to my first experience taking part in basketball camps as another significant way to share my talents and message.

By this time, I had graduated from law school. Thanks to my coaching and sports background, my ties to the community and my reputation as a caring and trustworthy person, I developed a large client base and made a good income as a lawyer. But I quickly discovered that while law was a good way to make a living, it was tough way to make a life. I was disillusioned with the legal system and wasn't sure I was helping young clients improve their lives, as many were already so hardened. I represented many who sat and listened to me but then would find themselves back in the system due to strongly entrenched bad habits. In addition, I found myself drinking more frequently and using alcohol to fill my own emptiness.

I got married and became the father of my oldest son, Jimmy. My marriage lasted a little over a year, and many of my friends would refer to it as a "regretful" time in my life, though I would always respond, "If I didn't get married, I never would have had Jimmy." Jimmy was my first and biggest incentive to stop drinking. I believe witnessing my mother and her life of caretaking and sacrifice led me to push for custody of Jimmy and the opportunity to raise my son as I was raised. Fortunately, I met with little resistance from his mother, and at a time when most fathers were seeing their children on an alternating weekend basis, Jimmy was with me all the time. I met my present wife, Kim, and when we married, she accepted Jimmy as her own, and we were blessed with three more sons: Casey, Brett and Shea. It was Kim's love and encouragement that provided the ultimate strength for me to stop drinking for good and build our family together. I also needed her financial sacrifice, support and encouragement to ultimately make the decision to fulfill my passion and calling.

It was with Kim's full support that I realized I could make a much more significant impact working with younger children: I could impart those character traits I had learned such as kindness, selflessness, honesty, community, respect and responsibility to those whose hearts were most open. This would provide youngsters with a foundation to carry them through their lives. It was the germinating seed for what would become my *Future Stars* program.

I began a slow transition out of law and into coaching kids. I continued to practice law by day to supplement my family's income and held basketball clinics for younger children at night and on weekends to feed my soul. At times I felt a struggle to perform my law job, as daily it left me unfulfilled and empty. On the other hand, the clinics allowed me to teach these younger children in an innovative and fun way.

As my son Jimmy grew and began his own sports experiences, I felt a need to pass on what I had learned through my early life and my coaching: Make the game fun, use age appropriate equipment, let everyone participate and interweave Life Lessons in the teaching of the sport. I would watch Jimmy's youth team play, and I saw how frustrated and unhappy some of the kids were trying to learn the game of basketball.

"They are too young for it to be stressful," I thought. "It should just be fun." This was my initiative to really get to work--to create a program for younger kids, boys and girls ages 5-9, that fit their needs by lowering the baskets and introducing smaller basketballs. The kids responded well: they just wanted to learn *and* have fun, and left sweaty, tired and happy.

This is when I realized I was on to something good—for both myself and the kids. It was a perfect fit combining my love of sports, children and an ability to pass on character traits I had learned as a child. Although the sports component was good, I soon began making plans to grow the program into something bigger and more meaningful. I thought about how the kids were friendlier to each other when they were coached age-appropriately, and how that camaraderie on the court improved everyone's game and friendships off the court. I began hand-picking coaches, who were selected to not only teach basketball, but were also trained to build character, foster spirit and promote teamwork. This ultimately became The Future Sports Stars Academy with *The Lessons of Life* program at its core. *The Lessons of Life* is a 21-part character development program in three tracks: Substance Abuse Prevention, Education and Personal Values. Each track consists of seven lessons, such as Kindness, Community, Health, Safety, Bullying, Sportsmanship, etc. Each lesson has its own visual aid presentation board and accompanying workbook which contains age appropriate homework assignments for each lesson. In conjunction with good conduct, sharing, kindness and listening on the court, each student is rewarded with various prizes for finishing homework assignments on the particular lesson. I use the sport they love as a "hook" to impart these foundational and valuable lessons.

The Lessons of Life teaches students to be the best person they can be. My faith and my life's dedication to kindness forms the basis of the lessons with morality at the forefront. The Academy is unique in that most sports instruction programs target older children and don't include the personal value instructional component. I believe working and molding younger children is the place to start when endeavoring to change the world and create a more caring and kinder place.

While my father was proud of my educational and professional accomplishments, he was skeptical of my transitioning out of law altogether. He worried about the loss of income and how I would support a family. I'm forever grateful that my father finally came to one of my clinics toward the end of his life. There, he saw how I was able to engage the kids in sports and "life's lessons" and how they responded to me. "You are really good at this. You should do this," my father said. That blessing has carried me through many times when the bills were adding up or when I encountered financially hard times and felt I wasn't able to do enough for my family.

With *Future Stars* up and running, I finally decided to sell my law practice. It was then that the principal at St. Joseph's High School in Trumbull, CT, offered me the position of Director of Athletics. Finally, I felt like I was where I was meant to be, working with young kids at my camp and teenagers at the high school during the day. As an Athletic Director, I was involved with every student-athlete in the school: attending practices and games, interacting with them and guiding them through their high school years. I learned early on that "kids don't care how much you know until they know how much you care." This premise fit my skill set perfectly. A sincere concern for their well-being, something which was a foundation of my personality and character as built by my family. This served as a daily opportunity for me to listen and teach. Each team participated in charities, food drives, Toys for Tots, visits to the elderly as well as the sick. This forum was a perfect opportunity to teach the concept of helping others, especially those who could do nothing for you in return.

It is within this book I share my experiences, my hardships, my joys and even my worst tragedies. The seed for this writing has been the theme of my life, which was to share with my children how being nice and being kind can lead to an enriching and beautiful life, returning riches far greater than any material gains and how it sets an example for those around you. I only hoped my legacy would be the passing on of these ideals and character traits to the future generations of my family, but now I believe it is something more people need to learn so we can improve as a society and make "nice" the standard of being.

Sometimes it isn't even that people aren't nice, it's just they are paying attention to their own behavior and not looking outward. Take a look at what's happening in many aspects of our society today. Sports contests seem more about personal celebrations, grandstanding and protests than healthy competition and team effort. News networks are being cited more frequently for false reporting and intolerance for opposing views. Social media is so full of trolling and so many do not use the THINK ethics standard (Is it True? Is it Helpful? Is it Inspiring? Is it Necessary? Is it Kind?) when commenting on others' posts. I have seen many so focused on getting into the perfect college and choosing top professions, which can provide them the most material wealth, but in doing so; they forego the many opportunities to step out of themselves in an effort to help someone else.

These represent just a few of the disturbing trends. Selflessness and thoughtfulness is now often replaced by selfishness. What do you think enables negative and damaging activities like these to flourish? It's the lack of *caring* and *character* of the people involved. It's a failure to realize how living in a kindness-driven life can not only help others but can help you through some of the inevitable hardships in your own life.

This was clearly apparent at the worst time of my life--and my families' lives. As I stood next to my son Jimmy's casket and as thousands of people waited hours to simply pay their respects to him and our family, I realized how from my grandparents, to my parents,

17

through my wife and I and directly to our children that this ripple of caring and kindness we created came back to us as a tidal wave of love and respect. It was at that moment I realized it was time. Time to share this message of love, hope and kindness practiced by those before me and lived so well by my son.

The tenets within this book, if read by many, can lay a groundwork for a better, more civil world. A world where kindness creates a wave of good acts, the benefit of which is not always apparent but is always life and world changing.

More than ever we need to promote ethics, morals and character by reminding people about the power of *honesty, generosity, respect, responsibility, courage* and so many more undeniably *good* traits. The list of virtues is long and with each new one you adopt as part of your personality, the better you will perform in your relationships, career and society as a whole. I believe with each new person that commits to living a character driven life, we take another step closer to reversing the negative trends we see playing out around us every day.

The purpose of this book is to highlight some of the people and stories in my life that made a difference and to show, that situation by situation, how character becomes a choice you make. There are a number of specific character choices I made which are illustrated by personal anecdotes in the pages that follow. It is my contention that most, if not all of them, flowed from one deep seeded belief. This belief created a life I wouldn't swap for all the riches in the world. It made me who I am and graces me with all that I have. It's *Kindness-* and this is my *Kindness Formula*.

Part I

Kindness and Character Development

The world is full of good people.
If you can't find one, be one.

Nishan Panwar

*The level of our success is limited
only by our imagination and
no act of kindness, however small,
is ever wasted.*

Aesop

Kindness

First and Foremost

"You cannot do kindness too soon, for you never know when it will be too late."

~ Ralph Waldo Emerson

Early on a Saturday morning in 2004, right after I left my job as a lawyer to pursue coaching and my Academy, I was making my usual Starbucks coffee and newspaper run while contemplating the direction my life had taken. I wondered, 'Was I making a conscious effort to do good for others first, but foregoing opportunities for substantial financial gain that would benefit my family? Was this worth the satisfaction reaped from my chosen life's path?' On the horizon loomed college tuitions, future retirement, bills and unanticipated expenses. Had I been irresponsible to myself, my family, and our future? Had I made the right decisions? Should I have remained a lawyer?

I quickly decided I shouldn't question myself or my values. I would continue to stay true to my beliefs and follow my own advice. I silently reaffirmed my personal *Creed*: Do not regret trading your money for memories and always do the most good for the most people, no matter the personal cost or expense.

Feeling more confident about my decisions, I walked into a convenience store and bumped into an old acquaintance who knew me back in my coaching days at the University of Bridgeport. He was a huge sports fan who could talk forever on the subject. When I first met him, it was at my camp. He had a son who was a struggling athlete and he enrolled him in my *Future Stars Basketball Academy*. On this particular day, he asked me if I was still teaching kids basketball and I told him I was.

He told me his greatest memory of my camp was during a game when my son Jimmy, who was on his son's team, dribbled over to his son and handed him the ball. My son had attempted to pass the ball to his son before, but the boy couldn't catch. Ironically, Jimmy was never known as a passer when he played basketball, but I knew Jimmy was that type of kid to give a hand off when needed. Jimmy was kind!

The man said he had never forgotten that kind act. Furthermore, his son, who is a successful businessperson today, told his dad it was the kindest thing anyone had ever done for him.

The father then walked away and I just stood there. I was so grateful; thankful for the message he gave me at the exact time I was doubting my choices in life. From that exchange, I knew I was following a worthy path. I was meant to help create those positive memories for others. It didn't matter if it was my son or someone else--acts of kindness spread from one person to the next person. I then realized you can never measure how much a simple act of kindness can positively affect someone. Trust it will have a lasting effect.

I further realized if I wanted to contribute something positive to the world, I must be courageous enough to be kind in a world that can, at times, be cruel. I had to be willing to bravely put myself out as a thoughtful, caring and generous person in this often hostile world. In a society where kind and nice people are often scorned or shunned daily, the most valuable gift will be your kindness. You will then see how empathy and compassion will flow naturally from your kindness. Furthermore, I believe wholeheartedly and repeat, the true measure of your life will be how kind you are to everyone, especially those who can do nothing for you in return.

To help my children achieve this goal I would share the following adage with them, *"you don't have to be friends with everyone, but you should be friendly to everyone"*. Friendliness is the simplest form of kindness. A smile to a stranger, holding the door for someone, listening attentively when someone speaks to you; be it a teacher, classmate, co-worker or the cashier at checkout. They may seem like insignificant gestures but they are not. In fact, a smile or a hello at the right moment could actually make someone's day. It is why I always stressed to my children that when they speak to someone, they should convey a feeling to that person they are the most important one in the world at that particular moment. Be that someone who makes everyone feel like a somebody!

Yet too often, many people do not put friendliness and kindness into practice in their daily lives. Looking at your cell phone, acting impatiently in store lines or cutting people off in traffic are the most popular choices. Impatience and our own "busy" lives filled with feelings of self-importance move us to defer those acts of kindness. Living with such unfriendly, unkind attitudes and actions might not only hurt someone's feelings or cause real physical harm, but could also inflict harm on the offenders themselves.

Kindness will improve the world, and the best thing about kindness is that it's free. It comes from your heart. You release it with an expression of words and actions. If you see someone looking sad, talk to them. If you see someone in pain, share their grief. Sit with the lonely one at the lunch table, or talk to the quirky, shunned colleague at work. It doesn't take much effort to be kind.

In a society where people are bullied on a daily basis, you can offer an alternative, *be kind first.* Rather than judging someone, *be kind first.* It will help you understand their point of view. Rather than ridiculing a person, *be kind first.* It will help you comfort them. A simple smile or hello can brighten a person's day, and a heartfelt thank you can make them feel significant. Everyone on this planet just wants to be heard, and you can work towards achieving that, one person at a time.

As you succeed in your personal and professional life, remember you are part of something bigger. Everything you do and say has an impact on those around you. You are responsible for making the world a better place by helping people in need. Even those who may

Lesson to Remember

Kindness is an easy choice and always matters. It can brighten a person's day, and quite possibly change their life. Kindness should be given without expectation of something in return. However, you will be pleasantly surprised to see practicing kindness will bring unforeseen treasures into your life. *Kindness shown* leads to *kindness returned*. It works like a karma boomerang.

Personal Assessment

Do you make kindness a priority in your daily life, specifically in your interactions with both people you know and strangers? Do you practice what Booker T. Washington said: "A sure way for one to lift himself up is by helping to lift someone else."?

Changing the World Challenge

Make it a point to be kind to the next stranger you see. Smile, say hello, and maybe even ask them how their day is going.

Make an unnecessary but kind gesture to someone you know. Call, text or email them to let them know you are thinking about them.

Your mission is to do at least one kind thing a day for someone— whether it be someone you do or do not know. Hold the door, tell someone they look nice or are doing a great job. It doesn't have to cost money or even time. Kindness is free and can be quick!

As you do this daily, take note of how you feel afterwards.

Jim's sons, the original Future Stars

Jim teaching "Lessons of Life"
at Future Stars - his true passion

Selfless giving unto others

represents one's true wealth.

Jon M. Huntsman

Selflessness

Forget about "Me" for a While

As an Athletic Director at a Catholic high school in an upscale town in Connecticut, the act of selflessness is the lesson most often discussed in my office at work. I like to leave a candy bowl on my desk, and students regularly come to visit me and seem to enjoy the treats I put out. They are probably unaware I also use the candy bowl to teach an important lesson about sharing and selflessness.

Every once in a while, the candy bowl will be empty, and a student will ask me for a new piece of candy. I tell them that there's more candy in my file cabinet, and then I wait to see what happens. Most students open the candy bag in the drawer and grab a few of their favorite pieces and shut the drawer. You may initially think nothing of this, after all they politely asked for the candy. I choose another way to look at it. I see an example of a selfish act. I explain to them taking the type and flavor of candy you desire without first filling the bowl will leave nothing for the next person walking through my door. I ask them, "are you built for yourself or are you willing to think about others first?" It is inevitable when they return and the bowl is empty they first ask if they can fill the bowl. Lesson learned!

Harmless, I guess, but also a potential indicator that says a lot about a person's character development at this stage in their young adulthood. If you have been used to focusing on, and living, solely for yourself, you get in a habit of not thinking about the people who will come after you. You take what *you* want and need and move on. It's all about me. During these conversations with young people I pause them and ask them to try and avoid the words "I" and "Me" in their responses to me and ask them to evaluate how different it sounds. This realization allows them to adjust their thinking to factor others in their thoughts, works, plans and overall life.

Do they do it for glory or medals? I highly doubt it. They do it for you and me. They do it willingly, selflessly. They think about someone else's safety before their own. Of course, these are extreme examples of what being selfless is all about. These occupations are not for everyone and no-one expects you to also make the ultimate sacrifice as they do. But you can be selfless in other ways, small ways that make a big difference, just like the candy bowl test proves.

The candy bowl lesson is simply a barometer. The fact selfishness is more often the automatic and natural reaction demonstrates to me we need more parents, mentors and teachers to take responsibility for the character development of our children. Teach them kindness and selflessness. Better yet, lead by example. Act kindly and selflessly towards others and get involved in your community. Demonstrate as adults you believe we all have a responsibility to the next person "coming for candy." To my younger readers, don't use the excuse "no one told you" to think about others. Somewhere inside you have probably been feeling all along it's the right thing to do. Next time you get the chance do it, fill the bowl!

Lesson to Remember

Selflessness doesn't require a major sacrifice. You just need to remember to think of other people. When you live for others, you have a true sense of community and you will naturally act differently. You'll take the extra time to fill up the candy bowl for the next person who shows up in the office.

Personal Assessment

Can you recall a time in your life when you put someone ahead of yourself? How did it impact that person? How did it impact you? Keep in mind two important sentiments: *"Selfless Giving* is your *True Wealth"* and *"Selfless Living* is your *True Self."*

Changing the World Challenge

Do a small selfless act tomorrow. Next time you are in line in a store, let someone go ahead of you. If you are driving in traffic, slow down and let someone enter your lane. Remember to wave and smile! Factor others into your thoughts by avoiding the words "I" and "Me." Awake each morning thinking about others and not yourself.

The Candy Bowl

My world is composed of

takers and givers.

The takers may eat better

but the givers sleep better.

Byron Frederick

Generosity

Yes It's True, It is Better to Give...

One summer we were winding down a family vacation in Long Island and the night before we left to head home my family and I went to a small Italian restaurant for dinner. Funds were getting low and I had no credit card on me and only had enough cash for a couple of days. While we were eating, I noticed a woman sitting by herself in a booth nearby.

She seemed to be struggling and obviously suffered from a type of handicap. She was asking the waitress questions about the menu and seemed overly concerned with the prices. After we finished dinner, I pulled the waitress aside and handed her $30 dollars, hopefully enough to buy the woman a meal, dessert and a tip. The waitress, a young girl from overseas, could not understand why I would do that for a stranger.

I explained to her my belief in helping others and she was truly touched. She told me her second job in town was in the bakery and before I left for home the next day I should stop by. The next day with the car packed and ready to head home I walked into the bakery and asked for the young lady. She wasn't there but two young employees asked if I was the person that paid the bill for the lady.

I responded "yes" and they told me what a nice thing I had done and handed me a big box of donuts and pastries. On top was a note from the waitress telling me she was returning to her country the next week and would never forget this random act of kindness and generosity. She assured me she would spread the word of this story in her country and would try to act in such a way herself. Although not expecting a return of the "favor", it surely reinforced to my children the value of a good deed. Legendary UCLA coach John Wooden felt "you cannot live a perfect day without doing something for someone who will never be able to repay you." I guess you can say this was a 'perfect day'.

The second story, which demonstrates generosity, was when I witnessed a sense of giving emerge in my children for the first time.

The school I work at, Notre Dame in Fairfield, Connecticut, had our newly-accepted students night and one of my former coaches, Josh, had his daughter present as an incoming freshman. He graciously asked how my boys were and we exchanged a few other pleasantries. Just as I thought the conversation was winding down it veered off on a new topic when Josh's wife Tracie interrupted.

She reminded Josh and I of an incident when their daughter, the new high school freshman, was little. Years ago, our two families ran into each other at Disney World. Their daughter was only four years old at the time and in a stroller. Tracie recalled how her daughter never forgot when my son Shea ran up to her stroller with a stuffed animal he won on the Boardwalk's Arcade games. He handed her the prize he had worked hard for--and overspent--to win.

Their daughter still has the stuffed animal to this day and she often wondered to her parents why someone she didn't know would give her a prize they had won. I couldn't help but recall the ridiculous amount of money my boys spent those days to win stuffed animals and basketballs. Those things were in and of themselves only worth very little but there was a higher value to each and every penny they spent.

Today I consider those things a treasure chest of generosity flowing from Shea and my other boys. You see Shea wasn't the only one who gave their arcade prizes away to other littler kids. It became a boardwalk filled with small children in awe and wonder as to why some strange little kids (and since their mine I can say it) would give away their prizes after the effort and expense it took to win. The lesson was a simple one. Always be quick to recognize someone may need or want something more than you. Be generous and share your good luck and good fortune-it won't ever be forgotten!

My kids knew stuffed animals and other toys weren't really that important to them but to that girl in the stroller and the other children on the Boardwalk, getting those gifts would be magical. Now could there be a better place for a little magic than Disney? My sons realized they would lose the toy, however other children would gain joy.

These are a just a few personal examples of how being generous through a kind act of selfless giving has come back to me and my family in unexpected ways, there will be others in upcoming chapters. The point is, and I have seen it prove out time after time, if you think giving away something means you have less, you're wrong.

It is my hope your character development accelerates with each additional kind and selfless step you take. As you witness *Kindness* become *Selflessness* in your life and vice versa, you will see *Generosity*, which is the focus of this chapter, taking a bit more effort and some sacrifice on your part. Regardless, *generosity* is the next logical character hurdle for people interested in changing their life for the better.

Generosity requires not only giving of yourself, but also giving up something of yours which is valuable. This giving should be selfless and as a theme arises throughout, without expectation of something in return. I remind my own children and students all the time, "If you are doing a good deed and expecting something in return you are doing *BUSINESS, NOT KINDNESS!*"

It could be your time or money or a prized possession. Generosity means becoming aware that your possession has a better use with someone else and then giving it to them without thought of a payback. At times it will be easy to be generous. Other times it will mean going "without" for the good of someone else. In those difficult instances, generosity and selflessness form an alliance.

The sacrifice for a generous act may be greater than an act of kindness or even selflessness but it can also be more fulfilling, and, though you do not expect it or look for it, often surprisingly the most rewarding. I like to use the above examples to show how kindness, selflessness and generosity worked in unison to give me and my family some of the most memorable and instructive experiences we ever enjoyed together.

If your life is focused on "things" and ownership, maybe you could consider yourself monetarily less "rich" at the moment you give something to someone else. However, you'll soon discover, as I have, that you are significantly more enriched. When that happens you will realize the true definition of your wealth and self. There will always be people who have more money than you. However, if you live a character driven life they may never be as "rich."

Lesson to Remember

If you get a chance to be generous with your time or money, do it. Give. It is its own reward. Something unexpectedly may show up in your life. Your life will be significantly more enriched when you give something of value to someone in need. If you are doing a good deed and expecting something in return you are doing BUSINESS, NOT KINDNESS!

Personal Assessment

Do you choose to be generous when the opportunity arises or do you make excuses and avoid the situation? Do you believe what UCLA coach John Wooden said: "You cannot live a perfect day without doing something for someone who will never be able to repay you."?

Changing the World Challenge

Next time the cashier asks if you want to donate a dollar to a good cause, say yes. It'll only cost you a little bit of money but will make you much richer in other ways.

Carnival games at the Boardwalk, Disney - generosity at work

football games and always cheerfully and enthusiastically supported his efforts. As a dad, it was a wonderful thing to watch my son help this young boy reshape his life's direction. Lao Tsu said, *a journey of a thousand miles begins with a single step.* That is exactly what was happening here. Although, in this case these two young men were taking that step together.

At prom time this young man was shunned again. He was not included in the large group of seniors who were gathering at the beach to take pictures prior to the dance. In support of his friend, my son decided to skip the tradition, one he saw as an exclusive ceremonial rite of passage. He had a better idea, a more compassionate one. Instead, Shea organized a few couples to skip out on the pre-prom photo shoot to join him on a trip to the boy's house instead. They would take their pictures there which created one more twist to the story.

At the last minute, my son's friends, the couples who said they would go with him to the boy's house, backed out. We assume they buckled to peer pressure and chose to stay at the larger picture-taking event. My son had a dilemma. He had a decision to make and, it would seem, a tough decision given the circumstance of all his *friends* now staying behind.

Should he honor his commitment and help this boy or also buckle under, go along with the larger more popular crowd? Shea was led by his newly formed sense of compassion, and opted to go with his date to his friend in need and take pictures with the boy and his date. Just the four of them. To me that's a picture worth framing. It's a picture of compassion.

After the kids took their photos, it was time to drive to prom. This young man did not drive so his mother and father were trying to figure out how their son and his date could get back and forth from the dance without their *parental* involvement. After all that would represent more ammunition for insensitive classmates that saw the boy as not part of the crowd.

My son, who didn't care about what others might say, did what was natural for a compassionate person. He volunteered to drive the boy and his date to the prom. As they were driving away, the mother had a tear in her eye and informed us that, because of her son's handicap, he had never been in another student's or friend's car. That act of kindness, compassion and selflessness rolled into one by my son, resulted in the single most exciting moment of that boy's high school career. The young man's father, a very prominent businessman, later told my son that he predicted him to be a great success in this world, while my wife and I already felt he was.

The above causes me to reflect on what George Washington Carver said, "How far you go in life depends on you being tender with the young, compassionate with the aged, sympathetic with the striving and tolerant of the weak. Because someday in your life you will have been all of these." It is my belief *Compassion* ranks right up there with *Generosity* in terms of costing you something to practice it. It can cost you *deeply*. But don't worry, it's a good thing.

Generosity's costs are easy to measure. How much money did you give, or time away from an activity *you* enjoy was sacrificed for the benefit of someone else? Those things can be calculated with the simple math of addition and subtraction. *Compassion,* however, is more complicated. To stick with the analogy we used for *Generosity, Compassion* is more like algebra than the basic mathematics we used above. There are formulas at work here. And they work within you.

First, you must have keen eyesight to see clearly enough to notice someone's misfortune. Our eyesight allows us to *see*; however, it is our heart which allows us the *vision* to see the essential things invisible to the eye. Thoreau said it best, "it's not what you look at that matters; it's what you see."

Second, you must be willing to reach out, to "touch" them by showing you care. Your ears must be wide open to hear them "speak," so you can identify what the misfortune is all about. Be aware, many times your eyes will have to do double duty and do the "hearing" as well. Often, I have found, suffering's details can be communicated quite clearly without words.

Finally, the last part of the formula requires you to "feel". The most compassionate people have felt great pain in their lives, and the more similar your problem and pain the stronger your compassion to the suffering. It is your life experiences, if you are humble enough to share, that truly comforts. *Your head, your senses and your heart.* Your heart is where the cost is felt. Felt in sorrow for someone's plight.

You have to feel pain to understand pain. Feel it right down to your heart. Your heart is also where great joy will soon be felt. A great joy and feeling of fulfillment will quickly and convincingly replace the pain and sorrow. Those good emotions become activated and grow as you witness the person you voluntarily *chose* to help show signs of improvement. Each time they laugh or expand their horizons, becoming more part of the crowd and begin joining in activities they previously shied away from, it will create satisfaction for you.

Another example of *Compassion* was taught to me by one of my coaches. He remembers as a kid his father often took him, his brothers and sister out on drives or to a fair, a game or to a hot dog stand for a bite. However, often his dad would detour along the way to pick up a neighborhood boy to join them. The boy's name was Kevin.

Kevin had few friends, was shunned and in those days was considered "a bit off." Over time, he said a funny thing happened. Kevin just became part of the group and furthermore the family became possessive and defensive if kids would point or laugh at him.

He believes his father was kind and compassionate through and through. Clearly, however, he wanted to be sure his children were taught to be as well. To be aware and to care.

So let me wrap up by first repeating the definition of *Compassion* at the beginning of this chapter. *"...a feeling of deep sympathy and sorrow for another who is stricken by misfortune, accompanied by a strong desire* to alleviate the suffering."

What does it take to *alleviate someone's suffering*, positively impact and maybe even change their life story and elevate their growth and success trajectory? You have to be kind by acting, then selfless by thinking and putting the other person first for a while, next be generous with your time, and last, be compassionate by *feeling deeply* about their situation. As you can see, the building blocks of character keep increasing but also keep working together.

Lesson to Remember

Just like generosity, there is a cost to compassion. You must feel deeply. Feel enough to act to alleviate the person's hurt, even if you can only offer a little relief. I like to remember George Washington Carver's important life lesson in particular: "How far you go in life depends on you being tender with the young, compassionate with the aged, sympathetic with the striving and tolerant of the weak. Because someday in your life you will have been all of these."

Personal Assessment

Do you just feel pity for someone you see with challenges or do you feel compassionate enough to help and act if possible? What do you see? Our eyesight allows us to *see*; however, it is our heart which allows us the *vision* to see the essential things invisible to the eye. Thoreau said it best, "It's not what you look at that matters; it's what you see."

Changing the World Challenge

Next time you encounter someone with a problem make an effort to translate your feeling of compassion into action. Reach out and help; alleviate someone's suffering.

Shea's Prom

We can complain
because rose bushes have thorns,
or rejoice because thorn bushes
have roses.

Alphonse Karr

Perspective
The Kinder Point of View

Once again, I will utilize a couple of stories from my life to illustrate the concept of keeping a proper perspective in life because things, events and circumstances are not always what they seem!

My sons saved over $2,500 to bring Eli, an English Bulldog, into our family. Eli was a great dog, content to sit with us and watch TV, take long rides in the car and sleep. Eli had one behavior that created an issue with me. When he would go to the bathroom outside he would only go a short distance in the backyard and do his business adjacent to our patio. As a result, he created "pee spots" of burnt grass on our lawn. I would constantly complain how poorly it made our yard look and wished he would venture farther away from the house so the spots would be less noticeable. I would spend my weekends and my money reseeding these areas only for them to return.

One day we all noticed Eli limping and we were told he may have a knee injury. We were not overly concerned when we brought him to the vet until the Doctor informed us he was limping due to bone cancer. A few months later we were forced to put Eli to sleep, a devastating time for our family. A few days later I looked into the backyard to see the spots he created and wished I could have him back, "pee spots" and all. I felt it would have been better for him to have destroyed our entire lawn and still be with us. You see a "blotched" lawn and "pee spots" are minor things in life, the proverbial small stuff. I realized we are confronted daily with "pee spots" of all kinds, those minor annoyances that consume space in our brain and waste our time and energy. I vowed, and asked my family to pledge, to try and not let these minor things bother us moving forward.

I sent the following to my family when Eli was put to sleep. It represented a spiritual perspective needed when life is hard to understand. It went as follows, "As you all know Eli was put to rest today. We all know he was put in our lives for many reasons and will never be forgotten. As always, my effort and words are to help us find sense and perspective to things so here goes:

Two traveling angels stopped to spend the night in the home of a wealthy family. The family was rude and refused to let the angels stay in the mansion's guest room. Instead the angels were given a space in the cold basement. As they made their bed on the hard floor, the older angel saw a hole in the wall and repaired it. When the younger angel asked why, the older angel replied... 'things aren't always what they seem.' The next night the pair came to rest at the house of a very poor, but very hospitable farmer and his wife. After sharing what little food they had the couple let the angels sleep in their bed where they could have a good night's rest. When the sun came up the next morning the angels found the farmer and his wife in tears. Their only cow, whose milk had been their sole income, lay dead in the field. The younger angel was infuriated and asked the older angel, 'How could you have let this happen!? The first man had everything, yet you helped him,' she accused. 'The second family had little but was willing to share everything and you let their cow die.' The older angel replied, 'when we stayed in the basement of the mansion, I noticed there was gold stored in that hole in the wall. Since the owner was so obsessed with money and unwilling to share his good fortune, I sealed the wall so he wouldn't find it. Then last night as we slept in the farmer's bed, The Angel of Death came for his wife. I gave her the cow instead.'

Remember things, events and circumstances aren't always what they seem!

Another particular set of life circumstances helped me obtain a proper perspective. When I was in college, and even after, I would go out with my friends and have a few drinks. I would wake up the next morning with a massive hangover, feel awful, and tell myself that I'd never do it again. A few weeks passed and I was fine. The hangover was out of my system. All of a sudden, another party would come along. I would rationalize and remind myself that maybe it was not that bad and I could give it another try. As usual, I would have a few drinks with my friends, and wake up the next morning feeling terrible. I vowed that morning to never drink again.

A few more weeks passed, and there I was at another party with a drink in my hand. I said that I would stop, but I didn't. The next morning, the hangover returned, and once again I swore off drinking. I was having lots of *fun* but was clearly losing perspective of why I was in college and later, my objectives for my job. My grades suffered and later my work. I wasn't responsible and let the pleasure of the moments take over a more important and larger picture. The "Hangover Theory," as I like to call it, can be applied in any area where we lose perspective. We all convince ourselves and rationalize poor behavior will be corrected "next time." Next time, we will be kinder, next time we will be generous, next time we will be compassionate, and next time we will spare others the pain our destructive behavior brings. Time passes, the pain softens and we REPEAT!

Ten long years passed and although it was clear I was practicing destructive behavior habits, I had not hit "rock bottom" and continued to deny I had a problem. I knew this cycle would continue until I not only *decided to change* my behavior, but when I *also acted* on my decision to change. I needed my inner voice, my conscience controls, to stop just *suggesting* things to myself but rather to start screaming them. I was forced to do this during Christmas time 1991 when I found myself sick and sitting in a hospital bed. Rather than enjoying the holiday with people I cherished, my health and poor choices led me to a bad situation. Each day I witnessed my oldest son, Jimmy, who was three at the time, leaving the hospital room crying and saying he wanted to stay with his Dad.

As I will elaborate in a later chapter on Faith, it was New Year's Eve when my relationship with a Higher Power gave me the strength to face a problem, refocus my priorities and perspective. Right then and there I turned the volume all the way up on my inner voice and found the strength to see very clearly that everything I was about to lose was significantly more important than having one more at the bar. It was no longer *fun.*

I knew I wanted to be a strong example for my boys and chose a path of sobriety. It took time, wasted moments and a serious illness but I decided my career and family would be better off without this cycle of hangovers, remorse and back at it once the bad memories faded. I delayed the *fun* for another day and another way. I had found my perspective and knew the future would be a lot brighter and rewarding for me now. In addition, as you will read later, my decision to choose a path of sobriety was an instrumental decision which later helped save the life of one of my sons.

It's common to lose perspective and forget about the things that matter. We make a mistake, say we won't repeat the mistake, and then repeat it anyway. It will happen. You can't try to fix your foundation in the middle of the storm and that is why you need to constantly recognize and be willing to work on perspective and your life priorities. It's during moments of weakness you should think about those "hangovers". Then you can refocus on what matters.

It has been 29 years from that time in the hospital until today. It has also been the same number of years of sobriety, faith, family and rewarding career milestones.

How does the way you see things, your point of view, as the dictionary describes perspective, shape your goodness and character? Just like Google maps provides a "Shortest Route," maintaining a solid sense of perspective provides an inner voice that guides your decisions. It acts as your conscience control, suggesting whenever necessary it's time to take a turn at the next life intersection.

Perspective removes any fog that may be clouding your view as to the greater good, higher calling or the more responsible action to take. Perspective focuses your vision on the proper, more accurate point of view. Some would define it as objectivity. Personally, I like to call it *Perspectivity.*

Lesson to Remember

Perspective is your inner compass and voice, guiding you to make better decisions, big or small. Listen for it. Keep a proper perspective because things, events and circumstances aren't always what they seem!

Personal Assessment

Do you always opt for immediate personal gratification at the expense of your well-being and others? Do you regret your actions, profess you will change and then repeat the destructive behavior?

Changing the World Challenge

If you struggle as a result of destructive behavior, substance abuse or addiction of any kind:

Use the next occasion where you sense you are heading down a familiar and damaging path to check your behavior. Slow yourself down, remind yourself of how badly you felt in the past, and try a new choice. See if you avoid the harmful and destructive actions.

Eli, the Bulldog

*Being honest may not get you
a lot of friends, but it will always
get you the right ones.*

John Lennon

HONESTY

Nothing Worse Than A Liar And A Cheat

From a very young age my father impressed upon me his strongest belief: "There is nothing worse than a liar or a cheat." It wasn't until later in my life where I became aware of some questionable behaviors of some of his closest relatives that I realized where this mantra originated. In fact, his feelings were so strong and his hurt so deep that he would relate to my mother his fears of me growing up with a tarnished last name. Years later upon my law school graduation, my mother shared the following with me and related how my success had made them proud for reversing this family reputation. The following are excerpts from the letter:

When you were six months old and the Olayos name was plastered all over the paper. Daddy said "I'll never be able to look people in the eye, my name is mud". I remember saying "Just forget that attitude, there's a baby upstairs that has to carry that name the rest of his life. At the time, who could foresee that 25 years later, you would make the name respectable and well-known. For that we thank you, because somehow we knew there is something special in you. The thing that is most outstanding is your awareness of the things that are unique in other people. Your leadership and example have made young men want to be like you. There is no greater tribute to parents than to have people say "If my son could be like Jim, I would be so happy and proud."

I cannot presume to take any credit for your achievements and abilities; because everything you ever did came from your own hard work and determination. When you were just a first-grader, and you saw a friend of yours, no matter how far away he stood, you always made sure you called to them and said "Hello". Your thoughtfulness then has grown to compassion for other people and through that you have become someone people are proud to know.

When you were six months old and the Olayos name was plastered all over the paper Daddy said, "I'll never be able to look people in the eye, my name is mud". I remember saying, "Just forget that attitude there's a baby upstairs that has to carry that name for the rest of his life". At the time, who could foresee that 25 years later, you would make the name respectable and well-known. For that, we thank you, because somehow we knew there is something special in you. The thing that is most outstanding is your awareness of the things that are unique in other people. Your leadership and example have made young men want to be like you. There is no greater tribute to parents than to have people say, "If only my son could be like Jim, I would be so happy and proud".

I cannot presume to take any credit for your achievements and abilities, because everything you ever did came from your own hard work and determination. When you were just a first grader and you saw a friend of yours, no matter how far away he stood, you always made sure you called to them and said "Hello". Your thoughtfulness then has grown to a compassion for other people and through that you have become someone people are proud to know.

As you can see, the value of your reputation and honesty were lessons I was taught at a young age. My family instilled the importance of these attributes, so much so it became one of the first lessons I taught my own children. It was even mentioned in my father's eulogy as the cornerstone of his being.

Even when I was young, probably around five or six years old, there was one question to which most everyone my age knew the answer: "Who chopped down the cherry tree?" Of course, it was none other then our first President George Washington. His choice to confess to his father in the face of punishment became the benchmark for the lesson-be honest whatever the consequences!

The cynics would say that's just a childish tale, old fashioned and doesn't really represent reality and how people act today. What they're really saying is that *honesty* has gone out of fashion, times have changed. Today's standard is often everyone out for themselves. Win at all costs, success is paramount, failure is not an option, even if you have to bend the rules and stretch the truth along the way.

We have become complacent and cavalier with honesty because we have lost sight of its importance. We have been told our individual achievement is all that matters.

Of course, individual achievement can be a good thing. But we must not ignore that it really depends on how you reach your goal. Dishonesty is never a small issue. If you start when you are young with "little" lies, the worst thing that can happen to you is you get away with it. Your dishonest behavior will grow and evolve into some very dangerous behavior. That has much to do with the concept of the increasing nature of life's consequences.

Directly tied into living an honest life is how consequences factor into your decision to be truthful. Every moral decision, every action, every word uttered has a consequence. As you will see unfold in later chapters, those who opted for dishonesty, or in my parlance "rule-breakers," suffered consequences based on their decisions. It is important to recognize that consequences become larger and more dire as we grow. When we are young and practice dishonesty we are usually faced with teacher or parental admonishment or maybe a short period without our favorite video game. As we grow into adulthood, our transgressions cost us a week without the car or being "grounded." If we fail to learn our lesson and violate any of the examples used during our adulthood, the consequences become life altering. Loss of employment, divorce and even the possibility of jail, in addition to my father's greatest worry, the loss of reputation and family name.

There are other examples of great historical figures who were known for honesty. There aren't any examples of dishonest people who were considered to be truly great. That's because dishonesty brands you. You can't shake it off or shower it away. If you're honest, you'll never have to remember what you said or did, whereas dishonest people always have to recreate their lies.

Let's break honesty down into three areas of your life where it is important: *social, business* and *spiritual.* You have witnessed how *Kindness* expands and grows to influence and anchor other character traits, you will similarly see that *Honesty* also expands and grows as your outer shield to guard against bad behavior.

First, your *social* and *civil life.* If you are honest, things you *won't* do will put you in good favor with family, friends, teammates, classmates and often most important authority figures. If you build a track record of honesty, friends and family will always trust what you say and rely on your advice. You will be valued and will always be able to find help and support from all these groups if you need it.

Teachers and coaches will sense or hear about your honest character and take you at your word at times when there is an infraction at school or on the team. It's a great feeling to be rarely under suspicion of wrongdoing and live with a guilt free conscience.

Second, in *business* you will avoid a bad reputation, as your honesty will guard against cheating your customers. A restaurant chain learned an expensive lesson when claims of foot long sandwiches were about an inch short. Sales dropped and reputations were damaged. Business executives who are honest would never allow these shameful business practices to happen. Just as it does in your social life, honesty at work helps you develop good business relationships, whether it be with your boss, your colleagues and/or your clients, allowing you to grow and flourish in your career with those dedicated to seeing and benefiting from your success. In business, as in life, it is important to surround yourself with honest people. As Oliver Wendall Holmes so aptly said, "put not your trust in money, but put your money in trust."

Third, *your spiritual life* can be tarnished by not following the simplest of Commandments: "Thou shalt not lie."

George Washington understood the consequences of dishonesty. He foreshadowed Ben Franklin who famously said, "Honesty is the Best Policy."

So, how do you adopt this best policy? To quote one of the most successful sales consultants in history, Zig Ziglar: "Honesty and integrity are absolutely essential for success in life - all areas of life. The really good news is that anyone can develop both honesty and integrity."

To Zig I say you only need to develop a solid footing of *honesty*. If you do and you enter the business world, you won't have to develop *Integrity.* It's there within you already waiting to be put in the game.

Lesson to Remember

There is nothing worse than lying. Dishonesty is never a small issue. "Honesty and integrity are absolutely essential for success in life-all areas of life. The really good news is that anyone can develop both honesty and integrity." There are consequences to not practicing Honesty for you and your reputation. You can ruin yours and other people's lives if you are dishonest. Always be honest. A personal gain may feel more important in the moment, but think about what will happen when your dishonesty is discovered.

Personal Assessment

Do you have the right friends? The right friends are those made through honest interactions. Is there something on your mind you need to confess to? Sometimes it's helpful to get something off of your chest and make an admission to someone you've wronged. Sometimes it's to just bring it to the forefront of your own mind and have a conversation with yourself about it. How has making a dishonest decision made you feel? What repercussions has it had? What repercussions could it still have?

Changing the World Challenge

Practice honesty and teach your family to be honest. Clear your conscience and free yourself from that guilty feeling by confessing, no matter how hard it is. You will thank yourself as soon as you do. From there, think the next time you find yourself about to make a dishonest action. Write out the people it could affect and the worst way it could backfire. Make the choice to be honest, even if it doesn't bring you immediate personal benefit. Trust it will benefit you in the long run. Set an alert on your phone from one year from today, reminding yourself of this moment in which you chose honesty. On that date next year, reflect on that choice and how you view it in retrospect. I find that most people who make a dishonest choice regret it in the future, but no one later regrets choosing honesty.

Jim's honesty role models - his mother and father on vacation with the family

*The difference between the
impossible and the possible
lies in a man's determination.*

Tommy Lasorda

Determination

Reap What You Sow

If you're going to do something, I believe you should put 100 percent of your effort into it. Treat everything you do like it's the most important thing you do, regardless of how insignificant you think it is. It all adds up.

My oldest and late son Jimmy learned about this on a typical Saturday in the summer. When he was young, he was serious about basketball. He often said he wanted to be "one of the greats." I encouraged his dream, but worried he failed to understand he had to work hard and practice every day if he wanted to make it come true.

On this one particular summer afternoon, Jimmy was lying on the couch in our family room watching television.

"How come you aren't outside practicing?" I asked. "I thought you wanted to be one of the greats." "I will I am going out in a few minutes," he said. I did not say anything, but knew that he had a choice to make. I went upstairs for fifteen minutes, and then returned to the family room. He was still on the couch watching television. "I thought you were going to practice."

"I did," he told me.

I realized in this moment that Jimmy would never be a successful basketball player with this mindset. I sat down and had a long conversation about the part hard work and dedication would play in his life.

During that conversation is when I also realized Tim Notke's quote needed an addendum. Yes, it's true that *"Hard work beats talent when talent doesn't work hard."* Also true, as I learned with Jimmy, is that hard work needs determination behind it when success does not come as quickly as expected.

Jimmy and I had our first *"reap what you sow"* conversation. I clearly explained to him that results in anything will be directly proportional to the effort and hard work you put into it and the determination you have to succeed at it. Those who really want to do their best will practice every single day until they have mastered the skill, and then they'll practice some more to maintain a high level of mastery.

Jimmy carried that lesson with him to the day he passed and achieved greatness in something other than basketball. He would find that determination paying off as he achieved his success through incredible and admirable hard work. After graduating college and, after suffering 29 application rejections to get into Physical Therapy school, he was finally admitted and earned a doctorate in Physical Therapy. He secured a great job in New York City doing what he loved. I know that conversation hit home because he later tattooed *Reap What You Sow* on his inner arm.

Another personal and family illustration concerns my youngest son Shea. He had the misfortune of suffering a torn ACL in his sophomore year of high school and as a result was forced to miss his Junior season of football, his main passion at the time. He entered the rehabilitation process with hopes he would play again. He prayed his dream of being on a college team would remain intact. He was determined.

He started the rehab process slowly and with little results. I contacted one of my former players who was presently a physical therapist and an athletic trainer who owned a gym in Greenwich, Connecticut. This facility was approximately 45 minutes from our house. My friend agreed to help. Shea went there with me to be evaluated and immediately developed a trust and rapport with his new trainer. He dedicated himself to his recovery.

Shea would either drive to Greenwich or to the train station where he would take the train ride and then walk the rest of the way to the gym. After his workout he would return the same way, a commitment of 5 hours per day. He was so determined he followed this pattern for a year and a half, six days a week. The determination, dedication and work ethic paid off. He was able to compete as a Quarterback his senior year in high school and now plays football at a Division I University. None of this would have been possible without his extraordinary effort and determination.

My son Brett was in a similar situation. He was on a Little League baseball team, travel teams and a State Championship High School team. However, on occasion, throughout his early career he would struggle with his hitting. Like most baseball players he would slump and, for whatever reason, couldn't get a hit.

It was obvious he was frustrated. He loved baseball. I could also tell he didn't totally grasp the need to work hard, dedicate himself and be determined to break this slump. I told him the same thing I told Jimmy, that he would have to assess his drive and if he wanted to be successful, the only way to improve his hitting was through practice and hard work. A lot of hard work!

To make sure this lesson resonated, almost every day after school, we would put a bucket of baseballs in the back of my car, go to the nearest field and have batting practice. We did this regardless of other social opportunities or if he was tired. His determination was being tested. Months later his persistence was proven more and more with each crack of the bat.

He had become confident in his swing. As a result, his batting average improved and his enjoyment of the game reached even greater heights. A further dividend was that Brett's work ethic was solidly ingrained in him. He saw firsthand his effort produced results. He continued baseball into high school and consistently went to the local batting cage to hit prior to games. His determination continued to pay off. Brett's senior year in high school he led off the last inning of his last game with a base hit which turned out to be the eventual winning run. This hit and eventual run propelled them to the State

Championship. I'm sure if you asked him if that day alone was worth all the hard work, he would surely say—yes!

If you are one of the younger readers of this book, you have probably reached an age when there are activities, clubs and organizations or sports teams of which you want to be a part.

Older readers also see goals to be achieved. A career change, learning to fly an airplane, writing a novel or lowering your handicap on the links may be your current dream. For young and old alike, I think it is wonderful to set your sights on something new. Learning, practicing, improving and expanding your horizons is invigorating and makes you more whole as a person.

Once you have established your goal, now the question becomes, 'How do you get there? What will be required of you?' There are a number of variables which will impact how that question will be answered for you as an individual compared to someone else who may share the same goal. For as many people as there are, there are an equal amount of paths to get to where you want to be, as everyone's journeys varies slightly.

The paths are dependent on certain factors. One is talent, for a particular sport or acting or music or whatever you are pursuing. Do you have talent in abundance? Maybe you were born with a great voice and only require a small amount of vocal training and development. If so, your path may be shorter than others wanting to become a singer. I say *may* be shorter, because other factors play a part as well.

If you don't currently have the talent or the skill set required to reach your dream, then you'll have to develop it. That's where effort and training and hours upon hours of practice are required. It may be grueling and may make some want to drop their dream altogether. If it is important to you, you will find a way, if not, you will find an excuse.

In either instance, whether you are supremely talented or need to develop it through hard work, *Determination* will be needed. For the gifted ones, determination will keep you focused and set goals to the highest of levels. For those who will have to labor a bit more determination will keep you from going off course or dropping out of the race. Determination keeps your eyes focused on the prize.

Another tip on achieving your objective is to tell people you know about your goal and your plan to pursue it. Having people around you who know what you are attempting gives you encouragement when needed, as well as some coaching or even potential training partners to push you when you aren't feeling up to your plan for the day.

My son Casey displayed the greatest sense of determination in battling and overcoming addiction. At a young age he fell victim to drugs and was forced at 18 to enter rehab while most of his friends were entering college. My own alcoholism was both a curse and a blessing in that I was compassionate to his problem and my eventual journey to sobriety gave him an example to follow. The road to recovery was not easy and not without relapse; however, his determination, as well as admitting to his family he wanted sobriety, gave him access to people who supported him and encouraged him on hard days. It was his own determination—sustained by support— that led to his eventual success, which saved his life and our family. Casey now works at the rehab where he found his way and has a hand in helping those in a similar plight.

Determination will be your greatest asset. It will give you strength when you are certain your goal is right and you want it so much you refuse to let anyone or anything prevent you from obtaining it.

The opening quote for this chapter from the legendary manager of the Los Angeles Dodgers, Tommy Lasorda, is good way to understand the power of determination. General Colin Powell put it a little differently, but the essence of his statement on the subject is equally powerful. "A dream doesn't become reality through magic; it takes sweat, determination and hard work."

The road you will travel to reach any goal is going to get rough at times. Without determination, at times you may think you aren't going to make it. With a strong will and a sense of focus and determination, these times will seem like mere bumps in the road.

Remember that quote from earlier in the chapter? "Hard work beats talent when talent doesn't work hard." I can tell you from experience this is true. This quotation was worn on the back of my son Brett's travel team practice gear. His coach, Manny Torres, was a former Major League draft choice and pitcher for the University of Alabama. He preached this credo and would always weave his baseball lessons into life lessons. We all may be passionate about certain things in life and we may even have talent for that passion. What is the final ingredient? Hard work!

Hard work is the reason why the most successful people are not always the most talented. You may not have been born great. But you are born with a certain amount of talent- use that to cultivate greatness.

Lesson to Remember

If you're going to do something, give 100 percent. Most things in life do not come easy. You need a strong determination to ultimately achieve your goals. Learning, practicing, improving and expanding your horizons is invigorating and makes you more whole as a person. Determination is a great asset. Keep Tim Notke's quote at the forefront of your mind when you are getting tired: "*Hard work beats talent when talent doesn't work hard.*"

Personal Assessment

When you set goals for yourself and don't reach them, do you quit? Are you setting unmanageable goals or do you lack the drive, determination and work ethic? Sometimes it's easy to blame and make excuses for why you aren't achieving what you set out to do, but write down a few reasons why you might have been the cause of your own failure.

Changing the World Challenge

For every task that you engage, be determined to complete the challenge and give your all. When you partner with someone on a project, make sure you both are determined to be successful. Write down something you have wanted. List the steps and tasks you completed to reach that goal. Calculate the reasons you were successful and apply those to other goals.

Brett with a big hit in the State Championship

Casey (on right) at Turnbridge Treatment Center

Jimmy's Graduation from Physical Therapy Program

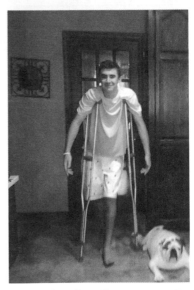

Shea healing from torn ACL

Respect for Ourselves Guides Our Morals; Respect for Others Guides Our Manners.

Laurence Stern

Respect

Learn it and Earn it

Many years ago, I was a member of a very successful grammar school basketball team. In our area the Catholic school teams were powerful and our team, St. Theresa's, was perennially one of the best. Our coach, Mr. Wallace, was different than many of today's parent coaches. Mr. Wallace coached for all the kids and not because he wanted to enhance the sports profile of his own sons. In fact, many seasons Mr. Wallace did not even have one of his own sons on the team.

If we won a tournament Mr. Wallace would treat us to Friendly's as a team in celebration of our success. We could order what we wanted, as long as we didn't spend more than two dollars. At the time, two dollars could buy you a hamburger, fries and a drink **or** the top of the line *Friendly's Sundae*. At the end we would walk up to the register and hand him our receipt for payment and he would comment on whether we stayed within his "budget".

Most of us would follow this rule, but always the same two players on the team ordered more than their share and went over the limit. The coach would comment to them and be irritated but accepted their receipts and paid them. I'll refer to these two as *Rule Breakers*, and although the dollar amount and transgression appear insignificant, it was nonetheless a violation of Mr. Wallace's trust and generosity. It was disrespectful.

As these two young men grew, they spent most of their lives bouncing from job to job, difficult relationships and always took the short cuts to avoid doing the right thing. As they became older the rules they broke became bigger and the consequences of their careless and defiant actions larger and more severe. Years later, I learned that one of them died of a drug overdose and the other had been unemployed and suffered health issues aggravated by drugs and alcohol.

This story is illustrative that respect and character, both taught or in this case failing to be taught, can be a guiding light or a roadblock when life and choices lead you down a certain path. Clearly, this moral compass can help you find your way in the midst of problems or even in the throes of addiction. Absent these character traits there seems to be little or no foundation from which to rebound.

It is important to recognize honor and respect as qualities to cherish and to follow. As I said earlier, my father would say, "The worst thing you can be is a liar and a cheat". You can add in don't be a disrespectful *Rule Breaker* as well.

I was fortunate to be raised in a family that took *respect* seriously. My father (obviously taught by his father) had some strong precepts that he never hesitated to remind me. Look people in the eye, shake hands strongly with a man; soft but firm with a woman, stand at attention and remove your hat at the National Anthem, call elders Mr. or Mrs. or Doctor until you are older and they invite you to call them by their first name, but then keep calling them Mr. and Mrs. and Dr. and on and on.

Often in today's culture, respect is misunderstood, misinterpreted, misused or, most sadly of all, missing. Furthermore, the word itself has even been abused. We hear only of its opposite (disrespect) and usually in street lingo or song lyrics, slang used unanimously to call out a personal offense by someone against you.

With little or no *respect* for the word respect itself or its meaning, no wonder it seems to have taken a break from society. You can see evidence of its void by simply observing the way people interact in most aspects of daily life. On the roads, shopping, at the movies and at restaurants. Almost anywhere you go it appears as if most are unaware of the existence and *humanity* of anyone they come in contact.

We need to get back to basics. If we don't, if we are not respectful and civil, how can we call ourselves a civilization? From the beginning of this book I have heralded *Kindness* as the basis, the foundation of most character traits. It holds true for *respect*. *Kindness* and *respect* are closely related. To respect another person is to acknowledge their right to exist. It doesn't get more basic than that. It would be very unkind if you didn't recognize the rights of others that you claim for yourself.

Respect means that you won't harm another person by silencing their voice. It means you'll allow them opportunity to express themselves, you'll pay them full attention, and you'll react with kindness to what they have to say, even if you disagree. A respectful person doesn't curse at someone else or laugh at someone else's suffering. A respectful person doesn't mock someone else's beliefs. A respectful person doesn't ridicule someone else's lifestyle choices. A respectful person doesn't derail someone else's dreams. I could go on for pages with more examples, but you will discover the others on your own if you just start by regularly practicing respect.

Paying close attention to others is something I try to practice regularly because it is a huge sign of respect. Paying attention to teachers, parents, clients, coworkers, children, friends, neighbors and strangers tells them you are interested, what they have to say and how they feel does matter. Paying attention makes others feel worthwhile and valuable. On this wavelength, I feel it is very important to know a person's name and try and make them feel as if they are "the most important person in the world" at that moment. There is no better way to respect someone's right to exist then to speak their name, thereby recognizing their individuality. As stated earlier, choose to be someone who makes everybody feel like a somebody.

I feel it is important to have respect for everyone, but most importantly respect your parents. If they are still alive, be grateful you have them and let them know it. I realized something recently that made me value my parents even more. The absence of my father forced me to take his place and be there for my mother, but in her eyes, I was still her precious child who she needed to protect. When my mother died, there was no one left to protect me. I was, for the first time in my life, on my own. It is a necessary circle of life, but it is difficult, and if I had known how difficult their absence would be, I would have tried to show my parents more respect and attention when they were alive. I like to say that *I wasn't truly a man until my father died, and when my mother died, I was no longer a child.*

I invite you to consider the phrase "respecting your elders" as more than just a slogan. You don't have to agree with everything they do or say, but you should always respect them when they are speaking. They've earned it. Your grandparents and ancestors have made great sacrifices for you, your happiness, and have contributed to society in many ways. The best way to show them respect is to take to heart what they have to say and express gratitude to them for sharing it.

Next are a few more vivid example of how a lack of respect can damage a society, harm people or even cost someone's life. The three exhibits refer to how people treat our *laws*, *rules* and *authority*.

First, the lack of respect for our *laws*. Crimes are committed daily because people have little regard for the law. But how about the majority of people who consider themselves law-abiding citizens? In other words you and me. Do you obey and adhere to the speed limit? Always? Didn't think so. Me either. It is a minor point I will admit, everybody has done it from time to time, and often no harm comes from it. You may even believe the speed limits are too low. However, if we feel the speed laws are unjust in our states, then we should lobby to change them. But we don't. Instead we just take the risk there isn't police radar around the next bend in the road and we continue speeding.

So, here's another one. Texting while driving. It is dangerous. It is against the law. It kills. Studies show it takes multiple seconds to refocus your attention back to driving when you look away to text.

Yet we see it more often than not, despite the deadly consequences, proving a good percentage of drivers still text and drive because they lack respect for the law or life, including their own. This is a premier instance of selfishness. There is a choice to read one's own message or to drive safely, and the selfish choice often prevails.

Second, there are also unwritten rules of the road we often disregard. These are more popularly known as common courtesy. We speed up when we should slow down to allow someone to safely merge on the highway. We tailgate and curse at drivers for committing the unspeakable sin of *obeying the law and keeping to the speed limit*. You may consider these violations minor offenses just like going a few miles above the speed limit.

How many times do we hear of incidents where the cause of a fatal accident was someone slamming into the car in front which had to make a sudden stop because they were following too closely? Or how often do we read of a road rage incident escalating into a confrontation that didn't end well because one of the parties had a weapon. There are volumes of reports of both of these type tragedies in the accident and crime logs all across the nation.

Third, is a lack of respect for *authority*. Examples such as disobeying a parent, disrespecting a teacher or disregarding a boss' directives all result in negative consequences. Respect matters.

We should show respect in the small things too. If you are a man, give up your seat to a woman. We all should relinquish our seat on a bus or a train to handicapped people and senior citizens. Pay respectful attention during the national anthem and take your hat off. Make sure to excuse yourself if you feel it is necessary to interrupt a conversation and excuse yourself if you happen to walk in between two people that are speaking. These simple acts of respect have gone by the wayside.

Respect the earth. Don't damage property. Don't litter or pollute. The earth is everyone's home, and it is your obligation to respect and preserve it.

Finally, respect yourself. Stand up for causes in which you believe. Present yourself to others in a way that makes you proud. It's possible to change the world, but first you may have to change yourself.

Respect can be boiled down quite simply. When I look back on my life, I realize there are two types of people: rule-followers and rule-breakers. The rule-followers are respected and respectful. The rule-breakers are neither. The legendary UCLA Men's basketball coach John Wooden stated it best when he said, "Discipline yourself and others won't need to." Have discipline and be respectful.

Lesson to Remember

John Wooden's quote is the lesson of accountability that I think is most important: "Discipline yourself and others won't need to." Always show respect to parents, elders, authority, our laws and our country. Those who show respect get respect. Have respect for yourself. Respect is earned.

Personal Assessment

Do you pay full attention when someone is speaking to you, respecting their rights and opinion? How do you respond to them? Do your words, comments and actions show that you fundamentally respect them?

Changing the World Challenge

Reverse the trend that people are unaware of the existence and *humanity* of others. We need to get back to basics. If we don't, if we are not respectful and civil, how can we call ourselves a civilization? Next time you see a veteran, fireman or police officer, thank them for their service. Next time you find yourself commenting on a social media post, ask yourself, Is This Thoughtful? Is it Helpful? Is It Inspiring? Is It Necessary? Is it Kind? If you can answer "no" to any of these, the comment is not inherently respectful. Don't post it. See how much better you feel when you don't tear down someone else.

St. Theresa's team
Can you pick out
the rule breakers?

*It is time to restore the
American precept that each individual
is accountable for his actions.*

Ronald Reagan

Responsibility

Show Up!

A sense of responsibility, like respect, is first learned at home. My mother was the purest example of responsibility. You'll remember her story: The oldest of 4 children, who, at an early age, was thrust into the ultimate responsible situation of having to care for her 3 younger siblings when she lost her mother to cancer and a short time earlier, her father to a work related accident.

By the time my older sister and I were born, 2 of these siblings were still living with us while they were attending college. My mother was raising her own young family while her and my father still tended to her siblings. It is clear to me now that along with responsibility goes a clear sense of personal sacrifice. Sacrifice can be seen in varying degrees in foregoing a trip to the mall or, like my mother, losing an opportunity to pursue her own dreams in exchange for providing and caring for her family.

In her case it was clear that responsibility often comes down to doing what you have to do versus doing what you want to do. My mother's sense of responsibility was strong and when she was faced with choices, she opted to make her family her top priority.

Likewise, when my boys became a part of a sports team or ventured off to college, I gave them all the same advice. First, *SHOW UP!* You have a class--show up; team meeting--show up! practice-- show up!; extra help--show up!; lifting--show up! This advice, if you ask them, has been the single most important ingredient to their success. Showing up serves two valuable purposes. By being present you will better understand your schoolwork, be better at your sport and create a consistent sense of accomplishment for satisfying all your responsibilities. In addition, it will show your teachers, professors and coaches you care, you want to succeed and you are willing to make every effort to do so.

The second bit of advice was "Work before you play!" In life, playmates are abundant, and this is no more evident than in college or even high school. You will always be able to find someone who is willing to distract you from your goals. Opportunities to go to the mall, the movies, play video games and even drink are a daily part of life. I have stressed to them to finish what responsibilities they have before taking someone up on these distractions. If you follow that advice, you will still have numerous opportunities later for fun. These "distractions" and activities will be enjoyed much more without the mental burden of knowing there is still work to do.

These lessons appear to have escaped today's generation as personal responsibility has been replaced with *blaming* and referencing that duties are *someone else's* responsibility. The absurd part of this blame game is the immediacy of it. Whenever something tragic occurs, far too often, people's first motivation, contrary to my mother's actions, is to look for someone to blame.

As with many problems we face, it is often good to get back to the basics. My basics are to always start with *Kindness.* I believe that applies to responsibility. Following these few basic rules and guidelines will give us the direction we need to become responsible people.

The first rule is no finger pointing or thoughts of casting blame, we are only going to focus on one person. You!

In addition, there are the two types of responsibility in addition to the rules above. The first is to be responsible for things that are expected of you. In this category, expectations have been placed on you by others, who could be your parents, teachers, your supervisors and coworkers, as well as your coaches and teammates.

Your responsibilities are usually spelled out for you in black and white. Your parents tell you your bedtime, when you need to be at the table for dinner and give you a list of your chores as well as other expectations.

In school you should know what time classes start. Your teachers give you reading and homework assignments and which behaviors are, or are not, acceptable in the classroom. In sports your coaches do the same. You must learn the plays, show up to practice, be on time for games and are often told to work on certain skills that may need some improvement.

Eventually job requirements are spelled out for you in terms of tasks, your schedule and quality standards to be met. Not being responsible at work can have severe and sometimes even dangerous consequences. You can lose your job or suffer injuries. When you have a family, consequences of failing your responsibility at work are compounded.

All these examples are like a responsibility roadmap for what others expect of you and there really isn't too much room for excuses in these situations. Even if you aren't certain of your responsibility, it's probably your responsibility to ask for clarification.

The second type of responsibility is to be a responsible person to and for yourself. In other words, be the best you can be and act responsibly when you do something wrong or you were the cause of an outcome being questioned. This can mean taking ownership of an action, apologizing and staying aware to make the best choices.

This second type of responsibility is the one I consider the tougher of the two. Being responsible to yourself is more challenging because, as opposed to responsibility to others, with this one, most times no one is looking. There isn't a teacher or coach around to spot your shortcomings and point them out. It's all up to you, your conscience and your character.

Being responsible to and for yourself means you don't look for shortcuts or the easy way out. It means you want to do the right thing always, especially when you can "get away "with less. The old saying *"character is the way you behave when no one is watching"* is a guide.

With conscience and character working in your favor, you'll be hard pressed to *get away* with anything, even if you think that's what you want to do. Either your conscience, fueled by your positive character traits, or guilt, will take you back to the proper course of action.

Guilt can actually be your friend in the area of responsibility, or it should be. It is your wakeup call and your alarm telling you it is time to atone for your actions and make amends. We all have, or at some point will have, a battle with guilt. Set things right. Then move on with a clear conscience.

Remember the way you handle *Responsibility* in your life will be seen by the world, and ultimately will define you, and as a result, determine your reputation.

Lesson to Remember

Be responsible! To yourself and others. A responsible person "Shows Up" and always puts their responsibilities before play. They can be trusted and counted on to do what they are supposed to do and what they're asked to do. Whether or not you are responsible will define who you are and how you will be judged. Responsibility is learned at home.

Personal Assessment

Pause and reflect on instances when you weren't responsible to yourself or others. What was the result?

Changing the World Challenge

Take personal responsibility and stop blaming others. Contact the people you failed, own up to your failure and apologize. If there is still a way to set things right, do it! You will feel better and be a better person.

Jim's Grandparents on his mother's side
(they died before he was born)

*Faith is about trusting God
when you have
unanswered questions.*

Joel Osteen

Faith

God's Plan, Not Yours

My faith is in God. Yours might be as well. I cannot help but feel throughout my life it has been God's hand which has sustained me and even *His* intervention that has saved me. In 1991 after an extensive illness, as a result of consistent destructive behavior, I was hospitalized and diagnosed with Crohn's disease, a serious stomach disorder. I was in the middle of a divorce and my son Jimmy was 3 years old. I was a lawyer at the time, was drinking heavily and surely was not taking care of my health. I was hospitalized on December 26th and, as I previously noted, Jimmy visited the hospital daily spending an hour and then left crying all the way to the elevator, "he wanted to stay with his Dad." This scenario was heartbreaking and lead me to great reflection as to the direction of my life. I credit Jimmy as being my first reason for my desire to attain sobriety.

It was 5 days later, New Year's Eve, and I was alone in my hospital room at midnight. With no immediate hope of getting out of the hospital, I turned to prayer. I made a pledge to God if he delivered me from this circumstance I would stop drinking, correct my priorities and lead a life that conformed to *His* will. At that moment there came a soft breeze through my hospital room and a sense of peace came over me. I no longer worried about my health or future and knew I had a greater calling. I have been sober for over 28 years and believed I have followed my calling of helping children and teaching Kindness. God's touch has been a constant since and although my life has been far from perfect, *He* has been always at the center. *I am a believer that no one can go back and make a brand new start, but anyone can start over and make a brand new ending. I hope to be a living example of this creed.*

I think the most difficult, maybe impossible, thing for anyone to accomplish would be to get through this life successfully and joyfully without belief in a higher power. By successfully, I mean you find your true *purpose* and *passion*, contribute to the well-being of others, find your perfect partner, feel fulfilled and live with a sense of inner peace. When I say joyfully, I mean you understand and accept your small part in a bigger picture and plan, a plan that will last beyond your time. It also means you found satisfaction in helping others, enjoyment in being kind and always did your best to take one right step after another.

Without belief in something greater than yourself and an inherited code of behavior, you would have no barometer to go by to distinguish between right and wrong. Actually, there would be no right or wrong. You would most likely believe it would be okay to live without guidelines, respect for the law or any true concern for others.

Why would you care about your actions, if there are no lasting consequences? For that matter, why then be kind, compassionate or honest or possess any of the other virtues? If you can get away with it, no one will know after all. With faith in a higher power you are aware there is always *Someone* who will know. Faith also reminds you there are consequences to your decisions and actions, the largest consequences of all-eternal ones.

On the flip side faith also supplies you with hope and guidance. Hope which can sustain us through some dark days and tough challenges, while faith's guidance is something we can rely on and seek daily--I live by faith!

Therefore, being a strong believer in God, my religious faith is important and even necessary. I believe faith in a higher power enables you to see the world more clearly, and from a new perspective. A daily reminder that pushes us toward a life of kindness and was a motivating factor for me to write *The Kindness Formula*.

As my wife and I have journeyed in this faith, we have been fortunate to attend a tremendous church with a Pastor who compliments our belief and our trust in God. We began going to this

Church when our son, Casey, was in the deepest part of his addiction and when faith was needed the most. We have learned from Pastor Frank Santora, people with faith may suffer setback after setback but one thing remains constant, faith and its partner hope. These will sustain you and provide the courage and strength to persevere. Rather than feel sorry for yourself and paralyzed by disappointment, you'll be able to get up and move forward.

I have selected more instances from my life where either I, or someone else in my family, faced challenges and difficulties. Thankfully we made it through these challenges. Each and every time, although it was never easy, it was one thing that fueled our strength, drive and determination-Faith. To quote Mother Teresa, "I know God will never give me anything I can't handle. I just wish He didn't trust me so much."

My youngest son Shea, faced some challenges in his favorite sport, football. As told in the *Determination* chapter, he tore his ACL in his sophomore year in high school and I have already spoke of the determination required for him to make a comeback. I didn't mention a further setback when, because of his loyalty to me, he transferred from a school where he was slated to be the starting quarterback of a State Championship caliber team. He came to my new school because I had left his old school for another position. Although my other sons were able to graduate from this previous high school, Shea's allegiance to me made it hard for him to stay. As a result, Shea came into a very difficult football situation and finished his long awaited senior year in high school with great disappointment. After all his hard work and determination to return playing, he was left with little to show for all his hard work.

He attended a few college camps and eventually was awarded a guaranteed spot on a Division 1 football team. When he received this opportunity, he showed up in my office and I told him, *"God's plan delayed is not God's plan denied."* I believe he had earned this opportunity as a result of his loyalty and faith. That saying became such an impactful thought to him; he had it tattooed on his side. He has had many moments to see God's plan at work, even though it wasn't on his terms or his timing. In addition, and more importantly, by going to that college he was fortunate enough to meet Margaret, a girl who is the definition of kindness and a person worthy of spending his life with.

St Augustine said, *"Faith is to believe what you do not see; the reward for this faith is to see what you believe."* If you still question the appeal and purpose of faith, consider the benefits and then consider the alternatives. With faith comes hope and the ability to accept tough times and move forward productively. With no faith comes blaming others, frustration, disappointment and giving up. You choose.

You may not realize a blessing you receive even related to a previous setback or lesson-God's plan at God's time! I could not conclude my faith journey without my own example of God's plan delayed. This example comes with a sad and tragic ending but again, it is my faith which allows me to get through each day. I told this story to my entire family on the occasion of my 60th birthday. When I was a young boy, I had 2 sisters, one older and one younger. I was a very active boy and loved to play sports. Although my sisters tried, I was often left to shooting a basketball alone or throwing a baseball against the wall. My imagination was vivid, but it couldn't replace my desire for a brother. I would "blame" my mother and complain to her I felt cheated not having a brother to play with. She even went as far to buy me bunk beds so I could have friends and cousins over for sleepovers. This was great fun but certainly not the same. One day I was telling someone this story of how deprived I was as a child when it dawned on me that God had a plan!! He never answered that prayer in my childhood but blessed me with 4 sons as an adult. The tragic event I mentioned earlier occurred on June 8th, 2019 when my oldest son Jimmy collapsed and died while participating in a triathlon in New York. Never in my wildest thoughts could I have imagined receiving God's gift of four sons and never could I think God would

take one of my boys from me so prematurely. God's plan, not mine-
-for better or worse. God's blessing of Jimmy in all of our lives and
the many lives of people he impacted must sustain me in this awful
time of grief. Dealing with this grief by focusing on helping others and
being kind to those around you is sometimes the only way I can stop
dwelling on this tragic loss. I believe as Jimmy's love and support will
lead me and his brother Casey through our sobriety, so will God allow
him to be the first to greet me at my time of death.

Lesson to Remember

Faith in a higher power reminds you that you are not the center of the universe; you need to care about others and do what is right. Faith also brings you hope that God has a plan for you. *No one can go back and make a brand new start, but anyone can start over and make a brand new ending*. Without belief in something greater than yourself and an inherited code of behavior, you would have no barometer to distinguish between right and wrong

Personal Assessment

Do you have faith in God or a higher power? Have you had an experience where God blessed you when you least expected it? Do you have the faith to persevere when others have hopelessly quit?

Changing the World Challenge

Research great people who have demonstrated faith and read their stories. Write down their quotes on how their faith helped them. If one of their quotes resonates with you, save it, print it out and keep it with you as a reminder to be faithful.

Jim and his 4 boys on their last family vacation to Montauk May, 2019 - one month before Jimmy's passing

Part II

Kindness and Personal Success

Nice guys finish first.
If you don't know that then
you don't know where the finish line is.

Gary Shandling

Introduction: Part II

In Part I of *The Kindness Formula*, the foundation for restoring civility to our culture was laid out. For those lessons learned to have any value, they must be put into everyday practice. We take the journey from *learning* and *preparing* to *living* and *doing*. In Part II, we will build upon this foundation.

As I showed with anecdotes about my early life and my children's early lives, the foundation of one's inner character is developed as a young person. The structure changes, and hopefully strengthens, as we grow older. Crucial decisions on which college to choose, if any, careers to pursue, raising a family, financial and other life-altering concerns complicate our lives. The choices we make, and the process we employ to make those choices, are critical.

Each of those situations has the potential to challenge what you have learned in this book. Thankfully, by using the lessons in *The Kindness Formula* you will increase your odds of finishing as a "Good Guy," reaching the goal and winning the right race, as Gary Shandling stated.

By following the lessons learned in *The Kindness Formula*, you will enhance your chances of reaching the goal line of life in two very important ways. The basics of Kindness and Character described in Part I will be embedded in you through education and example. Part II will show you how easily those good virtues can, and will, flow out of you and make your world, and that of your family, a much better place.

Also, in Part II you will learn how, when challenged, the basic character traits you learned in Part I evolve, expand and take on greater strength. For example, Honesty will be proven through Integrity in business practices; Determination is reinforced by Resilience when you fall short at times; and Generosity blossoms as you align with a specific Charity. By my definition, Part II will guarantee success.

By adhering to The *Kindness Formula*, your *caring* nature, and *character*-driven-heart, will guide you to make the right choices.

If you haven't got any charity in your heart, you have the worst kind of heart trouble.

Bob Hope

CHARITY

Graduate School for the Generous

Kindness, the preamble to *Charity*, creates an intent in your heart to help others. *Charity* is the execution of that intent.

The sacrifice of giving helps you focus your heart on the greater good no matter how small the act may seem at the time. It has worked for me more often than I can recount. This story tells of how charitable acts, no matter how small, can result in that *karma boomerang* in your life.

I like to call it "The Story of the Lollipop and the Ring." I know, candy keeps showing up in my life and lessons and I have no idea why but I guess it is my lucky charm.

I was again with my family in Disney World, and my sons were buying shorts at an outlet store. The shorts were expensive, but there was a buy-one-get-one-half-off sale they couldn't resist. I offered to buy the second pair for them and as we reached the cash register I noticed there was a bowl of lollipops. "Would you like to buy a lollipop for a dollar and donate to the children's hospital?" the cashier asked.

I noticed the mother in front of me had declined. Her daughter looked disappointed. It was then my turn in line. "I'll tell you what," I said, "Here's 10 dollars. Take 10 lollipops out of the jar and give them to the next ten kids in line." I believe whenever you have an opportunity to give, and you can, you should take it. Furthermore, if you have the means, give a little bit more.

When we returned to the hotel, my son Brett tried on his new pair of shorts. "Dad, come in here!" he yelled. My son showed me a gold *Tiffany* ring with diamonds. The ring was in the pocket of the second pair of shorts I bought him. "I'm the luckiest person in the world!" my son exclaimed. I then reminded him of the story of the 10 lollipops and pointed out it may not have been luck at all.

After attempting to find the rightful owner without success, my son researched the value of the ring. He discovered it was worth thousands of dollars. At the time he thought he would sell it and share the money with his brothers. You never know the effects of being kind to others and amplifying it with generosity. In this instance, that kindness boomerang returned with a treasure.

It is years later and my son still has the ring. His plans to cash in with his brothers has changed. He now intends to use it as his wedding band when he gets married to his high school girlfriend Lindsay. The ring will be a lasting symbol of their life goals to always be kind, selfless and charitable towards others. Lindsay is a very thoughtful and giving person so we all agree this is a much better plan.

Frank A. Clark once said, "Real charity is doing something nice for someone who will never find out." I'm pretty sure the next 10 kids who got into line after us and were given a surprise gift of a lollipop that day, never found out who gifted them the lollipops and probably didn't care. Thanks to my upbringing I didn't care they knew it was me. I was happy knowing the kids got a treat, the Children's hospital got a charitable donation and my children got a lesson in giving.

That is one small example, hearts refocused through charity and the better use of "things" for the greater good and benefit of others. And so this is *Charity*. The character trait of *Generosity* all grown up. It's your innate awareness of the importance of giving well practiced, trained, and honed over time. It is generosity matured, capable and ready to be focused on specific causes that aid the *least of us* but, importantly, are also dear to *your* heart. I say charities dear to *your* heart because I have a theory about causes that many share. The charitable causes you choose can often be indicative of your *purpose*. You will gravitate and focus on causes which resonate within your heart. Your focus in this regard will always determine the resultant time, effort and resources you will bring to this cause.

Acting on this focus and resultant cause, for most, is the issue. I'm sure like everyone, I have often found myself feeling a need to donate my time or money to a charitable cause. I hear a story of a stranger or someone who needs help and immediately want to rush to their aid. Sometimes it is time constraints and sometimes my own material needs that get in the way and, unfortunately, I cannot say I act 100% on these feelings. The purpose of this chapter is to come to a realization as to why we need to be ready, willing and able to act on these impulses more consistently.

Although I believe in being kind to those who can do nothing for us in return, I equally believe in being generous and charitable to others beyond my comfort level. Like *Kindness*, the act of *Charity* takes effort. We often "score keep" by measuring what benefit these charitable acts will provide. We also question whether the individual or group we are helping has done anything for us lately. This type of thinking is in line with our adage, if you are giving and expecting something in return, you are doing *business not kindness*.

Bob Hope's opening quote, which begins this chapter, serves the purpose of sending the message that a lack of charity in us doesn't just affect only those in need, it can wound us as well. However, the following quote from the Bible, Matthew 25:35 resonates beyond the heart and reaches down to soul of the matter of charity's importance in our lives. "For I was hungry, and you gave Me something to eat; I was thirsty, and you gave Me something to drink; I was a stranger, and you invited Me in."

I chose this biblical quote as the more significant launching pad for *charity*, and for a good reason. I believe it establishes a sound behavioral baseline for us to work from, because I think we need a moral compass to make the right life decisions. Being charitable is one of those life decisions.

Just as I believe we are all gifted with certain talents, I also feel strongly certain people and circumstances come across our paths in life for a reason. When they do - how do we react? What opportunities to make a difference in our little circle of influence do we seize upon? Out of the answers to those questions will spring the causes which you should consider aligning.

When you learn of the people, circumstances and "opportunities" that have crossed my path you should then see the rationale for the charitable causes I have chosen to support. There are a number of causes to which I contribute, however currently there are two particular causes most dear to my heart. I'll begin with the one which impacted me and my family both directly and indirectly.

I confessed to you I had been a drinker. A problem drinker. Thankfully, though, I am now 28+ years sober. I am proud of that accomplishment. I say that because I know how difficult it was for me to stop. I have also already told the story about my son Casey and his substance abuse problem. Gratefully though, through perseverance, faith and the blessings of God, my son managed to navigate it all and triumphed. As mentioned, he is not only clean, but now manages a Rehab Center and has dedicated his life's work to helping others suffering from addiction. His father, mother and brothers couldn't be prouder.

Through our own experiences, I realize how difficult it is for others to quit and am also aware the burden it places, not only on the addict, but also family and loved ones. The common thread of addiction that passed from dad to son affected all around us, and became a family cause and effort. This cause and resulting initiative started when a case manager of Casey's, during his rehab, introduced him to the therapeutic power of gemstones. Casey would collect various stones which assisted him during this troubling time. I even began to carry a few with me, in addition to my AA coin, each day in my pocket. When needed, Casey and I would simply reach into our pockets and roll the stones and coin through our fingers, a bit of support and comfort during trying times. This little exercise always eased his and my tensions and made us feel less alone. They also serve as a reminder of how fragile life and sobriety can be as that same case manager later suffered his own relapse and died of an overdose.

My wife, Kim took gemstones to a more sophisticated level by making beautiful bracelets out of them. At first, she just wore them for her own personal comfort. Then family and friends began requesting them. Kim was happy to oblige and her line of bracelets expanded. Many different stones and colors, each possessing different powers for varying needs were discovered.

Word of mouth grew also, as more and more people saw them and wanted to know where they could get one. Some of these people wore them for their own personal problems, or as a show of support for a loved one struggling with something. Others were interested in giving them as gifts and that's when the light of inspiration went on!

Why should the bracelets be limited to being an aid for only addiction? After all that is certainly not the only affliction people suffer from or burden families have to carry. Given our limited knowledge of psychology we were surprised at the number of issues we could name off the top of our head, issues we believed would cause someone to suffer mental anguish or physical damage.

Furthermore, when we combined our list with the numerous powers of gemstones Kim learned about from her research, we quickly filled a sheet of paper. In addition to dependency and addiction, we wrote down *grief, anxiety, depression, eating disorders, loneliness, diseases, physical trauma, mental disorders, and loss of a loved one, an abusive relationship* and a host of other *difficult life situations.*

These bracelets could help most people because it appears most *everyone* is suffering, or knows someone, who is suffering and *recovering from something!* That day *In Recovery Jewelry* was born. *In Recovery Jewelry —Support for whatever you are recovering from because everyone is recovering from something.*

Today we have our website up which features an online store and have received numerous orders from Hazelton Betty Ford, one of the largest Rehab organizations in the world, as they include and promote our bracelets as an aid to recovery. It is our goal and objective to be in a position to donate substantial amounts of the proceeds to addiction recovery as well as other worthy charities. This is truly a blessing.

Another example of how kindness would not stop tugging on my sleeve until I paused to listen was the opportunity for a children's charity that fit perfectly under the umbrella of the sports camp business I created.

My sports camps are for boys and girls 5 to 9 years old. There is a fee that, judging by my 20-year track record of success, is fair, reasonable and provides true value. Our sessions, held in both the suburbs and some urban locations, are usually sold out.

My dismay has always been the lower participation rates of the inner city kids. Whenever I can, I allow some of these children to attend for free. However, there is a cost per child associated and therefore free attendance had to be small and sporadic or I would be out of business.

Wouldn't it be the kind thing for me to do to find a way to help these kids on a larger scale? Therefore, I formed the *Future Stars Sports Children's Foundation*. Now, armed with a non-profit, I could apply for grants, seek sponsors to fund a scholarship program and do fundraising. Now I could now build up a reserve to help whenever a child couldn't attend because of economic reasons. In addition to the scholarships, the Foundation funds educational activities for kids.

I have similar examples from other family members and friends who dedicated themselves to charities because something related to them personally. Like Kim and I, they love to help and find their involvement extremely rewarding. Furthermore, whenever you witness progress and hear of success stories, the positive emotional feeling you receive is unmatched.

Always pay attention to the people and circumstances that cross your path. If you're open to it, you just might find yourself involved in one charity or another because it touches your heart's desires. I guarantee you will be glad you did. You can donate, give your time or give your expertise. It doesn't matter how you help a charity. Just be kind and help.

Lesson to Remember

Charity is the execution of Kindness. Real charity is doing something nice for someone who will never find out. Involvement with a Charity can be one of the most rewarding experiences in your life. You can give money, expertise or just your time.

Personal Assessment

Do you give to charity beyond your comfort level? Is there a cause close to your heart because it affects a friend or family member? If yes, can you help in some way? If no, can you help someone else's charity?

Changing the World Challenge

Focus on the greater good. Try to act each time a charitable impulse hits you. Give your time or money, no matter how little.

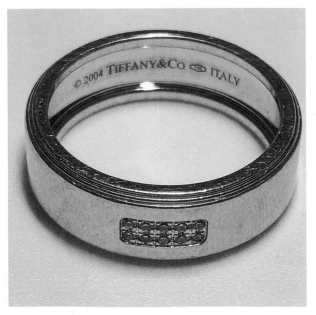

The story of the "ring" and the lollipops

Humility is not thinking less of yourself, but thinking of yourself less.

C.S Lewis

Humility

Always Be Humble and Kind

I truly believe there are aspects of *humility* tied and connected to its corollary, *selflessness*. This connection has exposed itself to my family and me through various life experiences.

My son, Shea, has grown up quite a bit since that day he gave away the prizes in Disney World as he later became a quarterback on the Sacred Heart University football team. I'm certainly proud of his sports accomplishments and love going to games and seeing him on the field and I'm even prouder of him because of what he does *off* the field.

I'm aware it is significant the day a football player receives a new piece of football gear or a new team sweatshirt to wear around campus. More than a simple article of clothing, it is a symbol of accomplishment and status. It represents they're among the chosen few who made it to this select group. They are on the team. Many wear it as a badge of honor and source of pride. On one particular day, my son didn't quite see it that way.

Shea was wearing his new sweatshirt he was given that day as he walked through the dining hall to get something to eat. He immediately noticed a young cafeteria worker cleaning tables. The cafeteria was relatively empty this morning and they were the only two in the room. My son had seen him before and could tell by his speech he had a certain handicap. When the young man saw Shea was wearing his football sweatshirt they struck up a conversation about football and, together as Giants fans, bemoaned the bad season they were having. Shea noticed as they spoke the boy kept glancing down to the varsity football sweatshirt. They continued talking and as Shea was about to leave with his food he asked the young man if he wanted his new football sweatshirt. The young man said "Really?"

Shea then said "It's yours" took it off and handed to the boy, whose shy smile quickly turned in to a beaming one and then a slight tear was visible. "Really?" was all the boy could say. Shea nodded his head yes, but then to cover every base, as Shea tends to do, also said, "You should wash it though since I had it on." The boy took the sweatshirt and asked Shea if it was OK if he ran and put it in his work locker. Being human, seeing other's needs; Being humble, not needing the prestige of wearing the new team gear; humility, being selfless.

I guess my son cared more about the young man in the cafeteria than being the *Big Man on Campus.* He showed *humility*. He knew he was on the team. He didn't need to prove it, display it or show off. That would be boastful to Shea.

The gesture also demonstrated he held on to his lesson from Disney about generosity. He knew it would mean more to the boy than him. Shea was selfless in that regard and so his compassion compelled him to lift his arms to take off the sweatshirt and give it away.

When you put it all together, he was kind. Kindness leads to some beautiful life moments.

As you can see this generous act was also him being his most humble self. He was humbled by the feeling that such a simple and obvious act, in his mind, could lead to such joy for another. The root of the word *Humility* is *humble.* For some reason, and unfortunately so, the word humble gets a bad rap much too often. We hear of someone's *humble abode* or are told to eat *humble pie.* From the sound of those phrases you can understand why people interpret the word in a negative light and conclude being humble is a bad thing. Actually, the opposite is true. Humility can be one of a person's greatest traits and character indicators.

Being judgmental, especially of others misfortunes and plight, is a trait we all fall victim to each day. My father, when confronted with judgmental people, would say, *"The shame is not in having problems, the shame is in doing nothing about them."* We constantly remind others that no one is perfect, but fail to recognize the imperfections in ourselves. Judging others for their problems and misdeeds is a pastime we have all enjoyed. This, we think, makes us feel better about ourselves; however, we should note what Ben Franklin said, *"You can't increase the stature of a small person by cutting off the legs of a giant."* It should be our mission to work on our own imperfections rather than attempting to feel better by judging the faults of others.

In addition to the connection of the two words *humility* and *humble* is the similar connection to the word *human*. In exercising humility we have to reflect on the fact we all have problems and difficult situations we face. The more of these human experiences we face, the more humble we become and less judgmental. This is never truer than with raising children. *We're all perfect parents until we actually have kids.* I surely became a much humbler person in the midst of facing my, my children's and my family's many human frailties. Being human and facing life's ups and downs will make you humble, decrease your judgmental attitude and cloak yourself in humility. Always maintain enough confidence to hold your head high and enough humility not to look down on others.

Many are also mistaken in thinking humble people are weak. Just as the saying goes *"Don't mistake kindness for weakness"*, living with humility is a vibrant and robust sign of someone's strength. It takes a special person to live that way. With no need for praise, or adulation or credit, holding their quiet satisfaction inside, they know they did the right thing or accomplished something to the very best of their ability. That knowledge alone is enough. As my sons played sports, I constantly reminded them that no one liked a bragger. If you are going to be good at something, let others be the one to talk positively about you. This may be considered confidence, but really, it requires a great sense of humility as well.

You must understand the confidence of humble people is something not shown or heard in bold claims and self-serving statements. Humility won't allow anyone who possesses it to turn confidence over on to its ugly side, cockiness. Cockiness is on display way too much today. You see it most evident in so called "professional" sports. One of my favorite sportswriters, Phil Mushnick in the *New York Post*, has weekly columns chronicling the lack of humility, team play, sportsmanship and professionalism in sports leagues today. Think about that. We have reached a point where there are enough examples of how *not* to behave to fill a few columns a week!

We see examples of it across the board. Baseball players who make contact with the ball no longer run to first base as their first instinct. Instead they stop and watch, to see if they hit a home run so they can call attention to their great feat. Every touchdown in football is now cause for personal demonstrations and dances, sometimes unsavory, that ignore the team and call attention to self. Basketball is the same, made baskets are typically accompanied by "hey look at me, *I* did that" gesturing.

Signs of humility are so rare they border on extinction. If the behavior of current athletes is supposed to somehow represent role models or heroes to today's youth, I pray kids turn off their televisions, or whatever device they use, and instead watch reruns from the past. There is no resemblance whatsoever to the sports heroes my dad watched, and I was raised to emulate. Somewhere along the line the concepts of sharing the glory, being good losers and gracious winners has been lost, taking team spirit down with it.

Another incredible example of humility I have witnessed is not by just one person, but in fact an entire generation. My father and uncles are the generation that fought in World War II. Tom Brokaw dubbed them the greatest generation.

Now what I am about to describe may also be true of previous generations who fought in wars, but I have no personal experience with them. Everyone I ever knew who fought in WWII had a curious silence about them. Despite the fact their lives were on the line as well as freedom, and the amazing fact they were as young as 17 when they left--they never talked about the war.

When I ask my friends about their relatives who fought, they told me the same thing about conversations related to their family's war experiences. Silence. Now despite the fact my peers and I discovered medals and commendations up in the attic or in the basement. Silence. Even when peppered with questions about fighting on the big one, the pat answer across the board was they *had a job to do, that's all*.

Sure, I guess there are probably exceptions. However, my experience was only with men, who as teenagers, many enlisting, risked their lives to protect their families and their country. Not for the glory or bragging rights but because their nation needed them.

This example came rushing back to me as I watched the funeral services for our 41st President George H.W. Bush. Most of the speakers referenced the goodness and humility of the man. They also highlighted a resume filled with wartime heroics, business, political and family successes. Many of his life accomplishments I had never heard before. Ironically neither did one of his political contemporaries who wondered why he never spoke of them only later to find his mother told him to never brag about himself.

Impressive man. Smart mother!

Thomas Merton said, *"Pride makes us artificial; humility makes us real."* The actions by my sons on the boardwalk in Disney World, giving the sweatshirt away at school and the greatest generation represented by George H.W. Bush, reveal the *genuineness* of their kindness and character.

You are building your life story with every choice you make, things you do and the way you act. As time passes it builds into a profile of who you are and, more important, who others think you are. Your final story will be written after you are gone, and maybe you think it does not matter at that point, but it does matter and you should care.

Bragging and belittling your peers who have not been as fortunate may feel like a way to build yourself up, but where will you really be if others are not genuine in their happiness for your success? Remember *"Talent is God-given, be humble. Fame is man-given, be grateful. Conceit is self-given, be careful."* Share the fruits of your success and stay interested in the successes of others, giving due respect and admiration for what others are achieving.

As noted, my son Casey, since his addiction and recovery, has chosen to *"make his mess his message"* and continues to work in the Rehab which saved his life. Tim Mcgraw puts it best in his song Humble and Kind, *"when you get where you're goin', don't forget turn back around and help the next one in line. Always stay humble and kind."* His song and lyrics are the National Anthem for this book!

Finally, here is a few things I have learned and try to remember each day when I have to make an important decision or decide how to act in a certain situation:

- Don't judge, you never know when their problem will become yours.

- People can learn from your story if it is a good one. It can help correct their behavior and change the paths they are on if you leave a good roadmap.

- If you have humility, you don't need to tell everybody how good you are, nor hear from others that you are good. Though you probably will!

- Celebrate but don't gloat--it's an ugly word and is uglier in action.

- Confidence can be positive, however if you don't keep it in check it will grow into cockiness. Cockiness can only grow into arrogance. Arrogance is not a good quality by anyone's standard.

- Humility, over time, will grow into class. Class, you may be surprised, is often what you *don't* do. Think about it.

Always remember, a mistake that makes you humble is better than an achievement that makes you arrogant.

Lesson to Remember

Humility is not thinking less of yourself, but thinking of yourself less. Pride makes us artificial; humility makes us real. Humble acts are the opposite of weakness. They strengthen your character, your relationships and contribute immensely to your legacy. Humility is an indicator of your character.

Personal Assessment

Are you judgmental? Do you celebrate or gloat? Do you *"help the next person in line?"* How do you act when you accomplish something in school or sports or on the job? Are you satisfied with your effort and work ethic alone, or do you boast and seek praise from others? If you boast, how much does this actually improve the way you feel about yourself? How do others respond to your boasting?

Changing the World Challenge

Strive to change the image of humility and it make it a positive one. Next time you are successful in any life challenge, make it a point to reject adulation. Praise and thank others for their contribution to the effort and for their help along the way. Always be willing to reach back and give someone struggling a hand!

#9 Shea playing football at Sacred Heart University

Our chief want in life is somebody who will make us do what we can.

Ralph Waldo Emerson

Mentorship
Teach the lessons you've learned

"To be inspired is great, but to be an inspiration an honor."

One of the greatest acts of generosity is to give so much of yourself to others you become their mentor. Of course, being selected the person that is an example and mentor to others can carry with it a critical responsibility.

My son Jimmy, before he passed, proved the true meaning of mentorship. My wife and I were seated at Jimmy's gravesite the day of his funeral when a woman and a young man approached us. She said she was one of Jimmy's patients and came from Brooklyn, New York with her son to the funeral to pay their respects. She was a NYPD police officer and went to Jimmy, a physical therapist, for treatment of her knee. During her treatment Jimmy would ask her about her family and her life. She related to him she was a single mother and had a son who lacked direction. Jimmy told her to bring her son to him after work so he could talk to him. Jimmy would stay, after completing 12 hour work days, and meet with the young man in an attempt to mentor him and help him find his way. It was at this time, by the gravesite, the young man, with a tear in his eye, said "Jimmy just gave me my first job." The mother then added, "He not only gave him a job, he taught him how to act, how to dress, how to greet people and to be on time." Mentorship at its best, for the kindest of reasons with no thought of personal gain.

I myself have been fortunate to have spent most of my adult life working with children from the ages of 5-18. In addition, I have had the greater fortune of raising 4 wonderful sons. These honors come with a great responsibility. A development of trust between the adult and the person they are affecting is required because no one will take criticism from someone they would not take advice from. I often say, *"kids don't care how much you know until they know how much you care."* The first step is to show a genuine concern and a sincere interest in others. This step was easy as it related to my own children but took time to develop with others.

A mentor of mine who played a very instrumental role in my development as a coach/educator is my uncle John Giampaolo, my mother's brother and someone I admired growing up.

My uncle was a prominent sports figure in the area but more importantly, he became a well-respected teacher and coach. Johnny "G" or Mr. "G", as he was affectionately referred to, had a tremendous knack of making each student he encountered feel important. He easily related and connected with children of diverse backgrounds and interests. The star athlete, the troubled teenager, the computer whiz, the artist-it didn't matter--I couldn't help but admire the way he treated everyone with kindness and had a reputation of being loved by all his students.

When I entered the world of education, my goal was to follow his lead and try to mentor and pay attention to as many students as possible. He was and is just a "good guy" and that was enough for me to aspire. Ironically, as my career developed in education I became known by my students as Mr. "O"!

I was lucky enough to have a mentor, my uncle, show up early enough in my life that it helped to steer me down the right path and gave me an example of how to express care and develop true relationships with each mentee.

I learned once people get a sincere sense of how much you care, you can then lead by your example. Most importantly, let your actions not your words create the example. It is important for others *"to pay attention to everything you do and less of what you say".* Those who look up to you will often times pay full attention to how you act, and it is these actions they should choose to emulate. I have been fortunate to have been considered a mentor to many of my former students, players and young people who have sought my advice. Being sober also has allowed me to mentor those in recovery from drugs and alcohol and provide them guidance and, once again, a good example to follow.

The textbook definition of mentorship is *the guidance of a person, especially by someone who is experienced in a specific situation.*

Mentorship is a life choice. It is rewarding to be a mentor, and hopefully life changing to the "mentee". Mentorship can be undertaken as a career in professions such as teaching or coaching. It can also develop on a more personal basis, for example, a corporate setting where one employee wants to help another seen struggling or just a friend needing guidance. You are never too young or old to be a positive role model or mentor to another.

A mentor is basically someone who offers their time and provides guidance to someone because they *care.* That's it. A simple one-word addition to what the textbook says, *care.*

Mentorship is the best way to release and let all those character traits you worked on in Part I flow out of you onto others. It is not only rewarding but satisfying. It almost sounds selfish in a way but the good feelings I have felt from mentoring someone is a main reason I gave up my law career to pursue coaching and education. It is when my *Passion* and *Purpose* became one.

A few of the following testimonials from some of my former players and students are evidence of what matters most to me as I was trying to inspire and mentor others.

"When you are feeling down look at the faces of the people (my players in a team picture) that you had a life changing impact on. Virtually all of them to this day tell stories of 'lessons' learned from being on that team. They may not always say it, but they are grateful." Keith

"Charitable actions, paired with his always positive outlook on life have impacted all of us. Even though many teachers feel we go to his office to skip class and eat candy, our true motivation to go is to spend time with our second father." Rob

"You made me realize things about myself that I didn't know and reminded me of the most amazing qualities in myself. You taught me to follow my dreams and passions, no matter what or who tries to stop me." Jordan

"Any problem I've ever had in life, you always seem to have a solution. I was always searching for someone to answer my questions and tell me what's right and wrong. You've given me the courage to forgive and forget and always be there for my family. You guided me into living a happy life regardless of the obstacles." Mark

"During your time here, you helped and changed the lives of everyone for the better. Before you gave us anything you first made sure we deserved it. You made sure, first and foremost, we were good people." Joe

These examples are present not to boast of my mentoring accomplishments but merely to show the potential impact we can have on others by taking time and effort to show others we care. These brief testimonials coupled with the "ripple effect"—how one's behavior impacts and shapes other's behavior--have contributed as much to my own "personal wealth", hoping my example would cause them to become positive role models for others.

If you have ever, or now desire to mentor someone you need to realize it is a privilege and you should take this responsibility seriously. Take the time to do it right. From my experience, from both sides of the mentorship equation, there are a few things that helped me. The following insights were gained from my research as well as thirty plus years' experience as a coach, educator and camp instructor.

First, stay focused. Remember mentorship is about one thing, helping someone discover things about themselves and advancing, not only in the given discipline at hand, but also advancing who they are. It is not about you, it is an exercise in generosity and goodwill.

Encourage first. Advise and correct behavior positively. Do not expect things will go smoothly all the time. Practice and demonstrate patience, not frustration or hopelessness.

Observe strengths and weaknesses early on in the relationship. Enhance and bolster the strengths as you work to improve on the weaknesses.

Break out to raise up. Good mentors take people out of their comfort zone and introduce new ways, new skill sets and new experiences so the person gains more comprehensive knowledge of the subject.

Be Collaborative. Ask questions. You might think you know everything needed to mentor another successfully; however, your perception may be different then the other person's reality. Find out what that individual thinks and ask questions throughout the process on topics such as progress to date. Make sure you listen to the answers.

Don't Give Up. My mother would often say to me, *"You water dead flowers."* But I always felt you should give everyone a chance to turn their lives into a success. People, especially young people, find their way at different times in their lives. Keep working and encouraging everyone, even the cases that appear hopeless.

It really doesn't matter what you chose as a career. *Lawyer, fireman, scientist, writer, teacher, coach, or chef*--I'm sure the best of them all had a mentor. The most *successful* of them will become mentors themselves.

Lesson to Remember

Mentorship changes lives. We all need one and all can become one by caring. Being a mentor is a privilege. Stay focused and exercise a genuine concern and interest for others.

Personal Assessment

Do you need help in something you are trying to accomplish? Do you have a skill or knowledge that can help someone you know? Being a mentor is a life choice. Have you chosen to be a mentor to someone?

Changing the World Challenge

Become a mentor! Lead by example and give freely of yourself. Recall someone who took the time to care about you who made a difference in your life. Reach out to them and say thanks! Think about how you can pay it forward and help mentor someone else.

Jim's Sportsman Award with his Uncle John -
"Johnny G" (on right)

*Harboring Anger and Resentment
is Like Drinking Poison
and Expecting the other
Person to Die.*

Saint Augustine of Hippo

Forgiveness

For Others _and_ Yourself

Robert Brault said,
"if you can't forgive and forget—Pick one!"

Compassion is understanding, as humans, we are prone to make mistakes. Our first reaction and response when we err is to blame someone else. I suppose this is understandable and natural to a degree. After all, in the current cultural atmosphere which places too much importance on _self above all_ and now _selfies,_ why would I, or anyone else, blame themselves? If something bad happens, we want to say it is another person's fault. Chances are, however, you will make a mistake or two at some point in your life, and something will be your fault. Why not be brave and acknowledge it? I have had to more often then I care to admit, but would not be where I am today if I did not.

As humans, we don't like to admit we're flawed, because then we would have to change our ways. However, the people who take responsibility for their decisions, realize they were wrong will be able to turn a stumbling block into a learning curve and personal growth.

Honesty and humility will go a long way to that end, but forgiveness will be equally integral to your development if you want to put the past behind you and move forward. Remember, as you move through life, you'll find that you aren't perfect and you'll realize you are human, which means you don't always do the right thing.

Forgiving yourself

In order to be a good person, you must swallow your pride and take _responsibility_. Own up to your mistakes or poor decisions, vow to do better next time. Remember there will come a point where you need to let it go. Don't harbor guilt. It will deter your advancement. Forgive yourself! This is not to say you simply mouth those two words, you are done, and you have absolved yourself and are now guilt free. It's not quite that simple.

Forgiving yourself is more than one action. It's an entire process and could take some time.

I think the best way to illustrate what I mean is to describe the process I went through years ago. Both of my parents play leading roles in this story, which illustrates the journey one must take in order to get to the level of realization that leads to self-forgiveness.

My father suffered from emphysema and had to use a portable oxygen concentrator for the last few years of his life. In 1999, on the last morning of our annual vacation to Montauk on Long Island, my father and I had an opportunity to have breakfast alone. My father was never a vulnerable person, but on this day, he decided to tell me he was afraid he did not have enough money for him and my mother in their retirement. I told him to not worry--that I would take care of them financially, and if something happened to him would take care of my mother. He was thankful and emotional at the same time and we finished our breakfast.

That same night, after we had returned to our condo from dinner, he was sitting peacefully on the patio enjoying the moment, happy and thankful to be surrounded by his grandchildren, when he slowly slumped over in the chair. Despite EMT efforts and other life saving measures he passed away the next day from what we learned was a heart attack. We had come to vacation as a family with him and left without him.

Immediate guilt overcame me. I shouldn't have taken him on a strenuous vacation, I should have been by his side when he passed, and I should have tried to help him more with his condition.

We returned home, I sold the condo my parents lived in, built an addition on my house and moved my mother in with my family. Most people wondered why I would take her in, but they were unaware of my promise to my father.

Fulfilling my promise eased my guilt and allowed me to realize I should forgive myself for those bad feelings consuming me concerning my father's death.

Unfortunately, the process repeated itself eight years later as my mother was diagnosed with dementia, and we were forced to put her in a home. When my mother passed away, I became acutely aware the ache inside me was not easing with the passage of time. In fact, it felt like it was getting worse. Deep down, I knew why. It just took a little time for it to surface and for me to own up to it. I was riddled with guilt.

It was only when my aunts and sisters would speak of the joy my parents experienced with their grandchildren and us on vacations and the love they had for us that my internal forgiveness process kicked into gear. The video was still playing in my head but suddenly the script had flipped. The scenes depicted a different man. I saw the times I *was* there for my parents and those were the times when it counted most. It was then, I forgave myself.

Forgiving yourself is a very important part of taking responsibility. Yes, it could be challenging. The process of forgiving yourself has two major components. First you have to look outside yourself and talk to those around you about your feelings. You may be pleasantly surprised to find out they see a side of the story you could be missing. Second look inside yourself, *watch the video* of guilt that has been eating away at you. Is there more to the story?

Forgiving others

Forgiving others is often even harder than forgiving yourself. If you want a life free of the thoughts of *getting even* or *revenge* or *wishing ill* on other people, you must forgive. Recall Brault's quotation, surely if we can't forgive, we should try to forget! Further, recall the wise words of St. Augustine which open this chapter, "harboring anger and resentment is like drinking poison and expecting the other person to die."

As world renowned financier and investor Warren Buffet states, "If a cop followed anyone for 500 miles, they're gonna get a ticket." Everyone is flawed. Throughout I give examples of my own imperfections to illustrate it would not be fair of me to hold others to a higher standard. It is better to acknowledge everyone makes mistakes and forgiveness must equally be part of the human condition.

If somebody hurts you, find it in your heart to forgive them. You don't earn bonus points by staying angry and holding onto bitterness, and you certainly won't be rewarded for any successful revenge plot. In fact, you'll feel worse. The best way to move past and heal after a painful transgression is to let go of your anger and sincerely forgive the person that caused you pain. Don't merely say you forgive, sincerely forgive.

Forgiveness doesn't mean that you condone the person's behavior. It means that you won't let it ruin *your* life. To forgive is to acknowledge that we're all human, we all make mistakes, and we all deserve second chances. To forgive is to choose to be happier and healthier by taking the high road towards inner peace.

A recent real life example is one of my many experiences on the road to forgiving others and releasing them for their offense. More importantly, it is my experience of freeing myself from stressful and damaging inner turmoil.

Prior to my current position, I was Athletic Director at another local Catholic high school. In fact, it was a position I sought out in earnest and gave up my law career to accept. The school also happened to be the one I attended. I was happy working there for 12 years and truly enjoyed witnessing the growth and success of its sports programs, as well as my relationships with the coaches and students. However, there were a few individuals who clearly went out of their way to make me feel I was no longer wanted at the school. Notwithstanding my good relationships with many of the students and staff, it became evident to me I was not welcome by some in charge.

Near the end of my time there I had arranged an assembly focused on substance abuse prevention. I had arranged for ex- NBA player Chris Herron, a recovering addict, to speak to the students. Chris was dedicated to helping others with abuse problems and had started a foundation to that end. It was his new vocation.

Although this pre-arranged assembly happened to fall on the day of my mother's wake, I still went to work and did not rush right out of the hall at the end of the presentation. Instead I took to the stage to thank Chris and also make a surprise announcement. These students and attendees knew me well and I was about to shock them. Caught up in the moment, I felt compelled to tell them that I too had reached a milestone. I was now 20 years sober myself.

They were certainly shocked. I also told them that anyone at any time should feel free to come to my office to discuss any problems they may be having. Unfortunately, I told them that today was the one exception, since I had to leave to get to my mother's wake on time.

While in my office readying my exit, one of the priests and a new school administrator approached me, saying they needed me to do something for them. I mentioned I couldn't now because of the wake, but I knew they were already aware of that, since they were in the auditorium at the time of my announcement. It should have been case closed but remarkably they persisted. Now I was the one who was shocked. A priest! Right then I threw them out of my office, told them to not even think of showing up at the wake and left. On the ride home I called my wife and told her I wouldn't be returning to the school next year. Soon after I left the job.

Over the next 2 to 3 years I held those two people, as well as the president of the school, who put them up to it, in contempt and felt there was absolutely no way I would ever forgive their insensitivity, nor would I ever even consider it. Then an internal process began in me.

One day when the incident crossed my mind for about the one thousandth time and I felt the anger rising inside again, I stopped in my tracks and paused my thoughts. I pondered who, after all this time, was really being hurt by my grudge holding? Were the priest and administrator thinking of me almost daily and wishing they acted differently? Were they raging with anger whenever they recalled the incident?

Most importantly, were they really such bad people that they were not allowed an error in judgment? Of course not. I, on the other hand, was suffering with a gripping resentment. Is that who I wanted to be?

Soon, after that inner process of debate, I noticed any recurring recall of that day became more and more about my commitment to the kids that I was there to help and less and less about the incident in the office. Forgiveness helped me release the bad and hold onto the good. It was even years later when I returned to my former school to participate in a memorial dedication for my son Jimmy and found I was at peace with being there and let my past feelings stay right there-in the past.

Some people probably believe I should have made them come to me and apologize, to *earn* my forgiveness. I no longer believe that's true. You should always forgive, regardless of whether or not the person who harms you deserves it. Forgiveness benefits you, and without it, you will be miserable and angry for the rest of your life. Why let someone else's actions determine your fate?

When you forgive, you take control of your life and choose to be happy on your own terms. Forgiving is in no way, shape or form an act of weakness. Mahatma Gandhi said it more eloquently, "The weak can never forgive. Forgiveness is the attribute of the strong."

Be strong because there is no greater power than the power of forgiveness!

Lesson to Remember

Forgiveness is a freeing action. It can free you from undeserved guilt and stressful grudges. Learn to take personal responsibility for your mistakes. Forgiving others can be difficult but worth it.

Personal Assessment

Are you in control of your life? Are you happy? Are you holding grudges? To forgive is a choice we make for our own happiness. Is there something you did in the past and you have not yet been able to forgive yourself? Is there someone you can't find it in your heart to forgive?

Changing the World Challenge

Choose one of the questions above, go through the process, flip the script and let go. Forgive, or at least forget!

Jim with his Dad and boys in Montauk
- the last days of his father's life

Gratitude is one of those rare things you get more of by giving it away.

Edmund Wilson

Gratitude

A Grateful Attitude

In 2012, Casey was in a rehabilitation center in Cape Cod, Massachusetts and was not doing very well. The therapist had prescribed a cocktail of medications which made him ill and plunged him into a deep depression. We received a call they were taking him to the local psychiatric hospital for treatment and observation. My wife and I were devastated, and our worry levels were at their highest. We contacted a long-term treatment center called Turnbridge in New Haven, CT., and they informed us a bed would be available in a week. In the meantime, while in the psychiatric ward, Casey met an elder Harvard-trained Psychiatrist who took a liking to him and counseled him numerous times a day. The doctor decided he did not need the medications prescribed and began to order them slowly discontinued.

We went to the hospital to visit and informed him he would have to stay a week before he could go to Turnbridge. My wife and I arrived early and noticed, adjacent to the hospital, a snack stand at the dock for the Martha's Vineyard ferryboat. We walked over had lunch and then entered the hospital. The visit was difficult. Seeing our son in this environment, surrounded by severely depressed and mentally ill patients, was heartbreaking. He was not pleased to be there for another week awaiting the move, but he had no choice and had to accept it. We left him for the long, sad ride back to Connecticut.

Casey entered the Turnbridge program and thankfully he thrived in the program and even had taken a job there two years later. During the early stages of his sobriety and employment, one of his co-workers invited him away for the weekend. We were glad, but worried. The day he left I received a call from Casey and was nervous to answer. He told me he was at that same Martha's Vineyard dock eating at the snack stand. He was waiting for the ferry and, unbeknownst to us was heading to his friend's house in Martha's Vineyard. He then told me he could see the window of his room in the psychiatric hospital from the dock, bars and all. He said he would often look out the window at the Ferry and wonder if he would ever enjoy a vacation like that again. You could clearly sense the gratitude in his voice. Not much I could say at that point, I got a little choked up. I mustered up, "Have a good time." And he did. This story illustrates the connection of Perspective and Gratitude. You need to borrow from what you learned about perspective in order to start building a foundation that can build a life of gratitude.

Gratitude has unique powers. If practiced correctly, it can unleash a powerful energy in you. This dynamic inner source of contentment stretches and releases outward from you to the betterment of the world and the people around you.

Eventually it returns to you from everyone it touches, assuring your supply is never depleted. Gratitude can also be a powerful source of concrete and measurable change in your life. Whether it is disappointment with your job, finances, or relationships, focusing on gratitude can replace the dissatisfaction with hope and accelerate the promise and realization of better things to come.

I often encounter stressed high school students, with their minds on college applications, finishing high school, figuring out their career paths, economic uncertainty, etc. My first response is to inform them these are all good and productive worries. I follow with an exercise where I paint a scenario where the above "stressors" are replaced by the following: You are told by your parents college is no longer a viable option due to financial circumstances, and that you have to drop out of high school and get a job to help your family. In doing so, you sacrifice your career goals, temporarily or permanently. I then ask them which of the two outlooks is more stressful. They obviously say the second so I then remind them to be grateful for the "stress" in the first situation. Finding a perspective that allows for gratitude helps them find a joy that they have these opportunities and feel more appreciative towards their parents and what they do for them.

As we move forward to explore levels of thankfulness and things to be thankful for, let's first define how *gratitude* differs from *appreciation* or a simple thank you. Those are important concepts too, but gratitude is a couple rungs higher up the ladder. Let's start with a simple *thank you*. At the conclusion of all of my camp sessions I remind the campers to be *grateful* and ask them to thank their parents for not only signing them up but making sure they had sneakers and their uniform, ate breakfast, and were able to attend a camp that costs money. This is high on our *Life Lesson* priority list, because if you can't be thankful, it becomes hard to possess all the other character traits previously mentioned.

Sometimes a *thank you* is ritualistic or in many ways a requirement society puts on us. Walk through any Hallmark store and you'll see aisles full of *Thank You* cards for various occasions. *Thank you for your Wedding gift, Thank You for my Birthday Present, Thank You for attending my Graduation, Thank You for being my friend.*

Thank yous, either sent by card or verbally, are important, but when it happens only because the *thanker* feels they *have to do it*, how much can it really mean? It becomes just another chore to be crossed off someone's to do list rather than a good opportunity to connect in a sincere and positive way.

Appreciation goes a little further. *Appreciation* can never seem or feel like a chore or assignment to be completed. True appreciation comes from within and requires something from you more profound than going shopping for the appropriate card. It is a real feeling and strong emotion the person you appreciate deserves a little extra effort on your part to ensure they know you are sincere.

For example, if you are in a group setting consider thanking the person and telling them how much you appreciate what they did in front of the group. This public act demonstrates to the person you consider them special.

Gratitude reaches even higher and goes much deeper. Furthermore, gratitude isn't necessarily just for or about another person. It is the energy you get when you are grateful for the world around you, even for things you don't like!

Acting grateful for things you dislike seems a bit odd, as I illustrated with the stressed high school student's story. Perhaps you are in a dead end job or do not have a job at all. These are both situations one would logically dislike, maybe even hate. However, a wholly grateful person would be thankful their out-of-work status gives them the time to approach a new job search full time. Similarly, gratitude enables unhappy employed workers to focus on the fact they are at least receiving a paycheck.

Coincidentally, the next two stories come from my summer camp I run for 5 to 9 year olds. I consider myself extremely lucky to have witnessed these two special people in the same place at the same time. I am equally gratified a couple of my children were working the camp that week and experienced it as well.

Smiling Rick

Each year at my summer camp one of my coaches, a special needs teacher, brings one of his students, Rick, with him to camp. Rick represents an advanced course in perseverance, acceptance, attitude and divinely gifted magnetism. As adults, we work hard to possess just one of these enviable qualities, yet have fallen short. Yet somehow Rick's personality overflowed with an abundance of all of them.

Rick, a 13-year-old autistic boy, can only makes sounds not words and often points to pictures or text in a brochure or towards other campers or scenes in progress at the camp. Those actions are some of the ways he communicates. However, his most compelling method of letting you know what he is thinking consists of the unmistakable wonder in his wide-eyed glances and the energetic glow from his smile.

While some of the other campers complained about the gym being too hot or their lunch too cold or any number of things, Rick just smiled. While campers complained of not enough time in laser tag, not enough tokens to play in the arcade, Rick did not and could not say anything. Instead he walked around and was just happy to be there and of course, he smiled.

I was in awe, of Rick and, also his parents. I couldn't help but think of them spending every waking second caring and providing for his every step. Everyone else in the camp, including me, would have had to be blind to not see how much better we had it than smiling Rick. What if I couldn't communicate? Would I still wear a smile on my face like Rick?

I wondered how my campers will leave their two week experience with Rick, who did all he could do each day just to be one of the group. Would they have a new perspective and sense of gratitude for all they were able to do? Would they be grateful for the simple gift of being able to joke around and have laughs with their friends? Would they see their speech as a gift, and now choose their words more wisely to uplift others rather than tear them down? I do know that each year upon Rick's departure from his 2-week stay all the campers yell his name and give him the camps loudest ovation. I think they learn something for sure.

Wheelchair Joe

At the same camp, there are about forty steps you must climb from the entrance doors up to the main gym we use. The last thing I, or any of my counselors felt when we faced them each morning was gratitude. Annoyance, anger and dislike for the stairs and also the buildings architect for that matter, were closer to the emotions and feelings we had.

But up we went and down we went three or four times a day as camp activities moved around to other parts of the facility. We did it, weren't happy about it and we certainly couldn't envision anything changing our opinion of the never-ending stairs. Enter Wheelchair Joe!

I met him a few years back after reading about him participating in a Tough Mudder event in a modified wheelchair. He was in a car crash in his late 20's and was told he would never use his legs or arms again. Since then he has worked at my Future Stars Camps and we have become friends. He always shows up at camp eager and enthusiastic, even giving Rick a run for his money in the smile department.

He is great with the kids and never has a regretful word to say or sorrowful look on his face. He wheels around the camp from station to station with pure joy emanating from everything he teaches and or to anyone he counsels. Joe often goes beyond the requirements of a counselor too. He brought his drone to fly for the kids and wore his Go Pro around his forehead as he whizzed around the gym in his wheelchair.

We tabbed him Wheelchair Joe amongst ourselves but in retrospect I think *Amazingly Grateful Joe* would have been a better fit. In fact, I'm not even sure Joe sees a wheelchair beneath him. Joe's attitude got me thinking about legs, and how we take them for granted. Imagine life without them. Life would be completely different and a whole lot more challenging for sure.

From the moment Joe showed up at camp, any time the counselors complained about climbing the stairway, I would ask them if they thought Joe would complain if he had the chance to make the climb. As for me, now when I enter the facility, I look up to the daunting flight of stairs that await and then down at my legs and say thank you.

With the perspective Rick and Joe gave us, how could anyone look at all the above simple tasks like walking, talking, getting to work, school and other obligations with a negative eye? See the positive in everything you do and feel blessed you can do them. Most importantly, be *Grateful!*

Lesson to Remember

Gratitude has a unique power which affects you and the people around you. Gratitude, being grateful, is an even deeper emotion than a thank you or appreciation. It is an inner sense of being, a way of life.

Personal Assessment

Are you grateful for what you have compared to others who have less? Do you focus on jealousy of others who have more? Do you keep certain perspectives which allow you to be grateful?

Changing the World Challenge

Write a personal note and send it to someone in your life for whom you are grateful. Tell them why. When you find yourself feeling envious of what others have that you do not, take a moment to reflect on the blessings you do have in your life. There is always someone with more, but there most certainly will be someone with much less.

Jim with Smiling Rick

Wheelchair Joe

One of the truest tests of integrity is its blunt refusal to be compromised.

Chinua Achebe

Integrity

Amazing How Your "Luck" Changes
When You Do The Right Thing

Integrity as a character trait is intrinsically tied to courage and leadership. I can think of no better situation and how integrity was displayed than through a story which again centered around my son Jimmy. He was 29 years old and was ready to leave for a bachelor weekend with 10 of his friends. They were prepared to board the van headed to Canada for 3 days when Jimmy called them all together. He said to them, "We all have great wives, girlfriends, and fiancées. Don't do or say anything this weekend that disrespects yourself or them." They all looked at each other as if to say, "Who is this guy"? They were prepared to go on a wild guys weekend, and he had the courage and character to remind his peers how to behave. Ultimately, Jimmy was respected for being the moral compass of the group and an example of integrity for them all.

My father would have been so proud of him at that moment, for his many lectures on honesty would always be reminder of the benefits you reap for truthfulness and having and maintaining a good reputation. He was a firm believer, as have I become, *you reap what you sow*, meaning you benefit from your good works. He never failed to say, *"It's amazing how your "luck" changes when you do the right thing."* The learned assumption was the positive result had nothing to do with "luck," but was rather a direct result of taking one right step after another. This saying is now a family mantra and has helped teach my children the trait we now all value: *Integrity.*

Integrity, that character trait which complements and reinforces the virtue of *Honesty*. Integrity, as defined, is the quality of being honest and having strong moral principles. Another way to look at it is honesty is what you believe is right, integrity is how your actions consistently prove that belief.

This was ingrained in me throughout my childhood and upbringing. I was not only taught to value the name given to me but to always make my decisions based on what was right, fair and honest. Just like *Kindness* and most of the character traits, *integrity* takes courage and great sacrifice. A short-term gain as a result of not exercising these traits will sometimes be tempting. However, often times *short term relief will lead to long term grief.*

Honesty is difficult to practice when you're young and gets tougher as you age. This is because as you get older you will find yourself in situations where temptation will approach you with "opportunities" that may compromise your integrity. It most often is a financial gain that presents itself to you as a byproduct of something you are already doing or comes to you as an offer from someone else.

The opportunity may look attractive to pursue. Someone may tell you there is nothing wrong with accepting the offer; *it's done all the time, standard operating procedure in the industry.* Temptation tugs at you to do wrong, you will start to hear your *This is Wrong* alarm going off. *Integrity is* how you respond to that alarm.

I had such an experience in my early years as an Athletic Director. One day I went to a local sporting goods store our school had used frequently and had a large revolving credit account. I would go in to the store, order equipment and they would bill the school. One day I went in with my sons and made a substantial purchase of equipment which, was obviously for them. When I approached the register the owner said, "Do you want to put this on the high school account"? I said "No, these items are for my kids, I'll pay separately". He then responded, "That's how all the other Athletic Directors before you did it." My honesty training kicked in immediately. I stated, "That's not how I do it. I'll pay". I never needed to have that conversation with them again.

Considering the amount of money I spent on my boys for sports, their proposed arrangement would have been a lucrative deal for me. These are often not easy choices to make for sure, but choose you must. I had the option of taking the gain while risking my job or pay for what was due from me and never risk the tarnishing of my name and reputation-a far worst fate.

It is situations like these when *Integrity* should be your guide. If you consider honesty to be your policy, think of *Integrity* as your track record of honesty in action when it is challenged. Integrity is your character resume. It can only be built over time, with each choice, until it becomes what you are known for and why you are trusted and relied on.

So remember, be honest, don't be a "rule-breaker", value your name and reputation and always try to take one right step after another and you will be amazed how easily your reputation and fortune will positively grow and how fast your "luck" could change for the better.

Lesson to Remember

The quality of integrity is respected. Integrity is something you build over time by always choosing honesty when confronted by temptation or peer pressure. It becomes your life's resume. Your *"luck"* will change for the better when you act with a sense of integrity.

Personal Assessment

How have you reacted when faced with a situation where your honesty and integrity has been challenged? When given an opportunity that seems too good to be true, do you evaluate the ethical implications and possible negative consequences?

Changing the World Challenge

Let integrity be your guide. Write a paragraph about what you would like to be known for many years from now. Then put it away until you have finished this book. Then go read it again. Would you make any changes?

*Bachelor party where young Jimmy (far left, top)
displayed leadership and integrity*

Do not judge me by my success,
judge me by how many times
I fell down and got back up again.

Nelson Mandela

Resilience
Shake It Off

From the time we were young, whenever we sustained a minor hurt or injury while playing, we were told to "shake it off". Not the most welcome response when you are hurt, but it attempts to teach you at a young age to get beyond the pain—to be *resilient*.

In illustrating some of the differences between *Resilience* and *Determination,* we find *determination* propels you forward, *resilience* picks you up and dusts you off when you stumble.

I like to think of *Determination* as your fifth gear, helping you generate more speed and energy when the road gets rough on the way to your goal. *Resilience* is what you call upon when the car runs out of gas and comes to a dead stop.

We all know life is not easy and we don't always get what we want. The younger you are, the more you think the world is there to serve you. As you grow you learn the opposite is true. Sometimes you will miss the mark and not reach your goal. Many people would call it failure but I do not like that word. I think of it more in line with the famous inventor who, whenever one of his experiments was unsuccessful, simply considered it as discovering another way *not* to accomplish his goal. He knew eventually by process of elimination he would find the formula that does work.

Don't think of anything you fall short on as a failure. Think of it as one more step completed in the process of achieving what you really want. Just because a car is out of gas it doesn't mean the car will no longer run, it just needs more fuel. Too many people in life would use that situation to totally give up, sit there and sulk. They become resentful and let a momentary stop change them. They become negative and see themselves as failures.

That's when *Resilience* is required. Resilient people immediately recognize they merely have to walk to the closest gas station, get a can of gas, refuel and get going again. *Resilience* also compels you to use the pause in your trip wisely, make the most of your "walk to the gas station" by using the time to reassess where you want to go when you fill up the car again. Do you want to go after the same goal as before? My son Shea did when an ACL injury brought his football career to a dead stop. My son Casey entered numerous rehabs and relapsed but kept going until he was successful. They learned at a very young age when things got tough—Keep Going.

I do suggest however that you recalculate your GPS to a different route or consider picking up another "driver" to help with the trip. Similar to how my son, Shea made great efforts and was determined to recover, even if it meant working with that distant and inconvenient trainer for more than a year.

Although you are told to get back on your feet and keep trying, you can't ever do it on solely on your own. We all need help. In 1983, I was the head basketball coach of a potentially very good team. I had a great rapport and relationship with this group of seniors as we had together been successful on the freshman and JV levels, and expectations were high as we entered their final year. Unfortunately, we faced early season adversity in some difficult losses, and although we remained focused and determined we needed something else. Then after practice one day one of my seniors paid me a visit. He was concerned I was getting a 'bad rap' as their coach and being blamed for our early struggles. It was a great gesture from a 17 year old; who also assured me the team was with me 100%. Moved by his words, I went home that evening and wrote a letter to the team, put it in an envelope, sealed it and wrote "Not to be Opened Until the Date of the League Championship". When I returned to practice the next day I gave the letter to my "trusted" assistant and told him to hold onto the envelope and bring it with him on that date.

From that point forward, we didn't lose. We made it to that championship game and I reminded the assistant the day before the big game to bring the envelope. He showed up the next day only to tell me he couldn't find it. We won the championship and I was only left to tell the story to my team of "The Letter" and relied on my assistant's acknowledgement of its truth, although he never saw the contents. My players, euphoric from the victory, understood somewhat, but I'm sure there were some doubters.

Months passed and one day my assistant called me to say he was moving his dresser and found the letter. I made a copy and gave one to each player. My captain had it framed as a reminder of the moment and the determination, trust and resilience the team possessed. We have our occasional reunions and "The Letter", as follows, and the lessons it taught are always a part of the conversation.

January 19, 1983

Dear Players

It is at times such as this when everyone comes to the forefront and claims responsibility for your success. The front runners and fair weather fans gather around the winners and attempt to convince you that they were sure all along you would come out on top. People patting you on the back were the same people sticking knives in our backs during our slumps and disappointments. This letter is evidence that when you doubted yourself doubted each other and doubted me there was someone who maintained a strong belief in your ability and character.

I am not going to say that I never had doubts. I had many times when I wondered if what I was doing was correct and whether I had misjudged the character of player on this team. Then one night after practice Brez, Frank and myself were sitting in the office talking. We were 5-4 at the time and coming off a disappointing loss to New Milford. Brez said something that made me write this letter. He was extremely frustrated about our lack of success and he was experiencing an up and down season personally. However, one of his major concerns was that he felt the team, and seniors especially, had owed me something and due to our failures I was getting a bad rap from the backstabbers, front runners and fair weather fans I mentioned previously.

from that night on I re-dedicated myself to making your season a success. People of quality rise above adversity and rise above people who cannot achieve, only criticize those who attempt to be successful.

I realized I was surrounded by quality people. I remembered 5 and 14 year olds walking into a gym for tryouts. Summer league at St. Joes, Gobbe St., Wilmot. Late night workouts at Wolfe pit and nights at no degree when everyone was swimming and drinking and we worked out. I could go on forever remembering and relating what transpired over your high school years but we know the things it took to get us where we are tonight.

Tonight you became adults. You battled the odds and refused to let others tell you what you were capable of. You achieved the unachievable and succeeded when the easy path would have been to fail. You proved to me once and for all that when something is right and you believe in people then you cannot fail. I believe in you. When you're all alone some night think about this moment and find strength in this success.

Congratulations 1982-83 Monak Panthers
W.C.C. Champions

Ace

January 19, 1983

Dear Players,

It is at times such as this when everyone comes to the forefront and claims responsibility for your success. The front-runners and fair weather fans gather around the winners and attempt to convince you that they were sure all along you would come out on top. The people patting us on the back were the same people sticking knives in our backs during our slumps and disappointments. This letter is evidence that when you doubted yourself, doubted each other and doubted me there was someone who maintained a strong belief in your ability and character.

I'm not going to claim that I never had doubts. I had many times when I wondered if what I was doing was correct and whether I had misjudged the character of players on this team. Then one night after practice Brez, Frank and myself were sitting in the office talking. We were 5-4 at the time and coming off a disappointing loss to New Milford. Brez said something that made me write this letter. He was extremely frustrated about our lack of success and he was experiencing an up and down season personally. However, one of his major concerns was that he felt the team, and seniors especially, had owed me something and due to our failures I was getting a bad rap from the backstabbers, front-runners and fair weather fans I mentioned previously. From that night on I re-dedicated myself to making your season a success. People of quality rise above adversity and rise above people who cannot achieve, only criticize these who attempt to be successful.

I realized I was surrounded by quality people. I remember scared 14 year olds walking into a gym for tryouts. Summer leagues at St. Joes, Goffe St., Wilmot. Late night workouts at Wolfe Park and nights of 100 degrees when everyone was swimming and drinking and we worked out. I could go on forever remembering and relating what transpired over your high school years but we know the things it took to get us where we are tonight.

Tonight you became adults. You battled the odds and refused to let others tell you what you were capable of. You achieved the unachievable and succeeded when the easy path would have been to fail. You proved to me once and for all that when something is right and you believe in people then you cannot fail. I believe in you! When you're all alone and feeling down some night think about this moment and find strength in this success.

Congratulations 1982-83 Masuk Panthers
W.C.C. Champions
Ace

Proof positive of what a determined and resilient group of people can achieve when faced with adversity, and this team captain has told me he's since used its lesson in business and with his own 3 boys.

Sometimes you fail to realize how your determination and resilience may come up short in achieving a given goal but assists you down the road. My son Jimmy is a perfect example, he went from playing basketball in high school to attending a small Division 3 school and playing on their team. He was the *first to practice and last to leave* and the hardest worker on the team--he had learned his lessons well.

Throughout his career, his playing time was never what he hoped or wanted but never altered his work ethic. He graduated and moved on to Physical Therapy school. On the day of his graduate school commencement, 3 years later, our discussions at dinner turned to college athletics. Jimmy said he was not sure all that hard work was worth it and he did not get much out of college basketball. I asked him if he was the hardest worker on the team and he said emphatically and indignantly "definitely"! I asked him how difficult and how much work was the 3 years of Physical Therapy school. He responded that it was very, very difficult. I closed by telling him although he never received gratification in basketball, it was his determination, work ethic and resiliency which helped him to achieve this far more worthy goal we were celebrating that day.

Resilience will become more important to you as you go through life. More sports opportunities will come but so may more times you'll be injured or not make the team. In business, expected raises or promotions may not happen. Socially, personal relationships may fall apart. Resilience is what you need when those things happen. It will be there to assist you to continue moving in the direction of your goals.

Lesson to Remember

Determination means you believe in your goal, will put in the effort and won't allow anyone or anything to stop you from achieving it. *Resilience* means having the ability to bounce back quickly when things do not go your way. Develop both! Remember to seek assistance when needed. You don't have to overcome obstacles all on your own.

Personal Assessment

Do you just sit by the side of the road and sulk when you don't reach your goal or do you know it's only a learning experience, "shake it off" and keep going? Do you label others as failures for not, at first try, achieving their goals?

Changing the World Challenge

When you reach a roadblock, think of a new path to achieving your dream. Make sure the goal and the avenue you are taking both makes sense and is challenging. All good things are worth hard work!

Jim's WCC Championship Masuk Basketball Team

The bad part about being called a good sport is that you have to lose to prove it.

Sy Presten

Sportsmanship

Play with intensity, Win with class

When I was 10 years old my grandfather, a Hungarian immigrant, came to my flag football league championship game. It was the first time he had seen me play. Our team was clearly outmatched and although I was able to score a touchdown, we lost 36-6. As the other team celebrated the championship, my teammates were crying over the defeat. I was not crying as I stood with my team, and this was not lost on my grandfather. He came up to me, said "good game", and then told me how proud he was of me that I maintained my composure and did not cry. He gave me the lesson that I will have many setbacks in life and I needed to find the best way to handle them. Some difficulties will require tears, but not a 10-year-old flag football game.

I also learned at a young age that respect and sportsmanship were values cherished by my grandfather and he had passed these traits on to my father. This was no more evident in my high school years as I often would forget my younger sportsmanship lessons and act out during games. My sophomore year in high school, I had a few contentious moments with the referees and even received a technical foul. At that particular game, where I was awarded the technical foul, ironically I had my best scoring game of the year and when I came home that evening, my mother greeted me by saying my father wanted to speak with me. I was sure he was going to heap accolades on me as the "great player" I had become. Wrong! He informed me my disrespectful behavior would not be tolerated and next time he would "drag me off the court himself" if I continued in such a way.

Sportsmanship and Respect are lessons which have carried with me throughout my life. So important in my education and the education of my sons, *Sportsmanship* became the cornerstone *Life*

Lesson of my sports camp, the most prominent of 21 varying character development initiatives.

Winning and losing, although associated with games, sports and competition, carries a more significant meaning as behavior clearly reflective of one's character. There are obviously thousands of examples of those who have practiced exemplary sportsmanship and unfortunately, many more instances of those who are "bad sports." A football player is ejected from his team's game after rushing for a first down near the goal line then violently kicking his tackler. He is suspended for two games by league authorities. A figure skater is attacked after a practice by an assailant attempting to break her leg to remove her from competition. The assault is ultimately traced back to her main challenger in an upcoming event. During a rematch between two boxers, one of the contestants bites a chunk off his opponent's ear and spits it out onto the floor. Then moments later, despite being caught and penalized, he attempts to bite the other boxer's ear again! The referee stops the fight, disqualifying the offender and awarding the win to his opponent.

I would like to first make a distinction for you between what I like to call "competitive spirit" and sportsmanship. Competitive spirit is the ingredient needed for an athlete, businessman, lawyer etc. to give them that *EDGE* and the *WILL* to be great. In my involvement with athletics over the years, I have witnessed varying degrees of this "spirit" and clearly know those with a high level have been more successful. This attribute often times comes with the negative perception that you "don't know how to lose" or "you are a bad sport". Competitive spirit is a positive attribute but it does need to be honed, or it can quickly cross the line of sportsmanship.

Many years ago, during my summer camp, my sons would participate in the contests, games and camp competitions. Being in charge of the camp, I was often put in an awkward spot, as my own sons would "lose it" if they didn't win. One day I was angry at one of my sons for their poor behavior and explained what was happening to one of the older coaches, who I considered a mentor. He clearly was not bothered by the behavior although he admitted it was over the top. He explained the concept of competitive spirit to me and advised me to "temper" the behavior, not kill it.

From that day forward, I became more tolerant of this behavior and worked with him in an effort to help him achieve a more balanced result. Respect of opponents, coaches, referees and more importantly, outcomes were things to consider. Body language was another important teaching point. Your body language and non-verbal displays are part of the process to achieve the harnessing of this competitive spirit. Finally, your words should always be measured (obviously not just a sportsmanship tip!). I often tell students that not every time you are spoken to by someone in authority you should feel an immediate need to respond. Sometimes a nod to a coach or referee, even if you disagree, goes a long way towards "tempering" behavior.

Unfortunately, these problems and resulting solutions are not limited to the competitors on the field. Coaches, parents, siblings and fans feel they're justified in joining in the bad behavior, when actually they should be the ones setting standards and demonstrating examples of how to be a good sport.

Sadly, we have seen this terrible behavior by "pros" and "adults" trickle down more and more to our youth, who emulate their "idols." Sports media compounds the situation by showcasing selfish acts, taunting, players fighting or arguing with officials as if it is acceptable and worthy of aspiring to.

It is as though nobody knows the importance of good sportsmanship but when you think about it, good sportsmanship is the *most important* element of the game. Of course, games and players get very competitive, that is natural. At times competition gets fierce, tempers flare and personalities surface, but that is exactly why sportsmanship must be learned in order to be utilized in those heated situations. Athletes should and must be reprimanded for unacceptable behavior. If not, there would be no guidelines or rules for others to follow.

But we can't learn it if we don't teach it anymore. Furthermore, who will be the coaches bold enough to buck the trend of the "me first" and "winning is everything" sentiment pervading every level of sports today?

It must start with today's youth, youth coaches and parents of young athletes. I am not saying you need to abandon that "competitive spirit" and the effort to win games, you just need to learn how to control this spirit and follow the basics of good sportsmanship and fair competition.

There is nothing wrong with winning because to become a winner you must practice and strive to be the best you can be. So winning is good, but winning the right way is even better. Tennis superstar Jim Courier said it best, "Sportsmanship for me is when a guy walks off the court and you really can't tell whether he won or lost, when he carries himself with pride either way."

Here is The Guide to Sportsmanship
as presented to the students at my camp:

Always play by the rules.
Treat others fairly and with respect when you play or coach.

Be a Good Winner. Celebrate but *don't rub it in*.
Respect your opponents, don't put anyone down.
Shake your opponent's hand.
Thank your teammates.

Be a Good Loser
If this time your opponent is better next time practice and do better.
It's OK to be disappointed, there will always be another game.
Congratulate your opponent.

Be a Team Player
Compliment other players.
Help someone if they get hurt. Be kind and care.
Don't complain or blame others.

Nobody wins or loses all the time. You could be on the other side next time, so treat your opponents how you want to be treated!

Lesson to Remember

Good sportsmanship is the most important part of the game. Without it, rules would not be followed, games would be unfair and fans would act out of control. You can exhibit good sportsmanship without sacrificing your competitive spirit.

Personal Assessment

What kind of sport are you? A team player and humble winner or are you selfish in games, a poor loser and a worse winner? Do you allow your emotions to get out of control while competing? Are you proud of your game behavior at all times?

Changing the World Challenge

During your next game or practice thank a teammate for their effort and if you lose the game, congratulate the winners and shake their hands. Similarly, if you are in business, congratulate the winner of a pitch, someone who gets promoted, or someone who gives a great speech or presentation. They worked hard for it, and if you keep working hard, it will one day be your turn to receive congratulations.

*Jim's Grandfather who taught
him about Sportsmanship*

SPORTSMANSHIP:

Playing by the Rules!

How to Win!
- You don't have to rub it in or celebrate too much.
- The loser knows you won, so does everyone else who watched the game!
- Enjoy the victory and congratulate your opponent!
- Nobody wins all the time.

How to Lose!
- Today the opponent was better, shake hands and compliment the opponent.
- No matter how you play today, there is always a game tomorrow!
- Nobody loses all the time.

Be a team player!
What Makes A Team Player?

Good	Bad
Compliment other players	Name calling
Think of team first	If someone gets hurt, you don't care
If someone gets hurt ask, "Are you ok?"	Walking away complaining and blaming others
Shake hands, WIN OR LOSE	Celebrate too much

Coach Jim says...
"EVERYONE HAS A ROLE IN SPORTS. YOUR JOB IS TO PLAY, LISTEN TO THE COACH AND DO NOT WORRY ABOUT THE REFEREE'S CALLS OR RULINGS."

Future Stars "Sportsmanship" Lesson of Life

Future Stars "Sportsmanship" Lesson of Life

A leader is a dealer in hope.

Napoleon Bonaparte

LEADERSHIP
"BIG DAY"

Leadership is inter-connected to the notion of *Responsibility* in that leadership requires determined, responsible and focused behavior and an outlook intended to help and influence others. We surely are responsible to ourselves; however, if this book has taught anything, it is the positive effect and results you are trying to achieve for others. At some point in your life you will be called upon to be a leader. It could be in a family situation or on a sports team, or maybe you will get peer pressure from your friends to do something you know is wrong.

Again Jimmy, during his short life and even shorter career as a Physical Therapist, became a leader and manager of 3 different New York clinics and demonstrated such a positive sense of leadership, it became a cornerstone of his legacy. At his wake, the people who worked with him said he would start each day by telling them all "it's going to be a BIG DAY"! or "let's have a day"! The combination of his infectious smile, his positive outlook and uplifting words brought a feeling to everyone that he would lead them through whatever difficulties they encountered and do it with enthusiasm. They would smile and try to make Jimmy's words prophetic by having that "BIG DAY"!

There is also a clear penalty to those who act as a leader. As the epic treatise entitled **Penalty of Leadership** states, "The leader is assailed because he is a leader, and the effort to equal him is merely added proof of that leadership. Failure of the follower to equal or to excel, the follower then seeks to deprecate and destroy-but only confirms once more the superiority of that which he strives to replace."

When you are in the position of leadership, you at times may create a feeling of unpopularity. Once again *courage* must prevail and, if your intentions are noble and well meaning, your leadership will result in respect. It has been said, *"You can't make everyone happy. If you want to do that, sell ice cream!"*

Some of you may interpret this to think a leader is just a boss with a fancier name. Let me say it another way to eliminate any confusion. A leader may be a boss. However, being a boss does not make you a leader.

The following details the differences between a Boss and a Leader. These differences, confirmed by many articles I have read and much of my experiences.

A Leader vs. Boss

Bosses want to control; leaders want to coach.

Bosses want people to fear them; leaders want people to respect them.

Bosses want to command; leaders want to collaborate.

Bosses shout orders; leaders make suggestions.

Bosses blame; leaders take responsibility.

Bosses engage in a monologue; leaders engage in a dialogue.

Bosses expect perfection and criticize mistakes; leaders encourage improvement.

If I could summarize all the points made above into one, it would be that bosses use power and leaders use influence to achieve a goal. First lady Rosalynn Carter stated, "A leader takes people where they want to go. A great leader takes people where they don't necessarily want to go but ought to be."

I have been placed in positions of leadership in my professions and chosen areas of work. As a coach, Athletic Director, lawyer and camp director/owner I have tried to put into practice the above leadership suggestions. I've learned you must be patient and understanding with those you wish to lead. Not all of those under your responsibility come with the same level of knowledge and expertise. Take the time to teach them the skills they need to know to succeed.

One of my father's favorite phrases was "It's not WHAT you say but HOW you say it that counts." Positive words in an acceptable tone will enhance your ability to be an effective leader. My Uncle Charlie was a great example of a leader who put this phrase to work during his 40+ years as a door-to-door vacuum cleaner salesman. When I was young, he taught me his leadership practice known to him as a *"curb conference"*. His function, in addition to sales, was to train the younger sales force. They would go to a house to demonstrate the vacuum cleaner and when finished would go to the "curb" so my uncle could deliver his critique of the rookie salesman. Uncle Charlie would tell me he always started the conversation with positive words. "The way you unpacked the vacuum and described it's parts was terrific!" My uncle found that starting with a compliment would positively affect the trainee and make them receptive to hear more. Once the trainee was listening, he would deliver his critique. The young salesperson was open to this constructive criticism on the heels of the compliment. I have practiced this "curb conference" hundreds of times in my interactions with people I was in charge. Work evaluations, problem solving, behavior changes and suggestions on performance all were met with a greater reception when they began with positive and complimentary words.

You will earn people's respect--and therefore distinguish yourself as a leader rather than a boss--by listening to them and taking their suggestions and ideas rather than dictating how everything should be done. You can also earn their respect by your willingness to share in the most menial of tasks required to get the job done. As Athletic Director, I never hesitated in sweeping the gym floor or picking up garbage on the field. I would say to my coaches under my charge that there is no job too small to help us accomplish our goals. In this regard, you must remember you can't lead anyone else further than you have gone yourself. Once my coaches and the students saw my willingness to perform these menial tasks, they began to follow my "lead" and perform them as well.

Finally, I believe one of the two greatest traits of a leader is the ability to take blame for situations and show people you are willing to be accountable for the failures and not just willing to take credit for success.

All of these traits determine how you will be remembered by the individuals within the group you lead. You will be remembered fondly by others if you start with *Kindness* and allow your other positive character traits to be revealed. Remember being a leader is helping people out of any situation to a better place. Sounds like kindness to me.

Lesson to Remember

Leadership is an important skill, often needed to solve some of life's most demanding problems. In your life, you will find many opportunities to lead. Leading well can bring you success and bring out the best work in those who follow.

Personal Assessment

Are you ready to be a leader? Are you a positive communicator with the patience to listen? Are you more of a boss than a leader? Are you willing to share in those menial tasks usually reserved for the newcomers? Can you withstand criticism that comes with leadership?

Changing the World Challenge

Be a leader and take your followers where they should go, not where they want to go. A good leader knows the difference. Next time you are in a group situation where no one can agree, take the lead. Use influence and suggestions, not power and control. List the facts and point out the consequences of different courses of action. Help others arrive at the best destination.

Shirt made by Jimmy's company honoring him after his passing

*The two greatest days of your life are
the day you are born and
the day you realize why.*

Mark Twain

Success

Love What You Do And Love Who You Do It With

What is success?

We all have our own idea of what makes a successful life. To some it is finding and pursuing our dream job or career. To others it is amassing the largest possible fortune and being able to obtain all the desired material possessions. For some, success is obtaining certain power or prestige in the community and perhaps your workplace as well. For too few it is finding your "soulmate" and keeping good friends. Finally, there are others who value their health above all else. Ultimately your goal is to find the proper balance of all the above.

Regardless of your choices and personal preferences, you will find happiness when you discover what you love to do and a greater satisfaction when you love who you are doing it with. These two critical ingredients, as the following will explain, are necessary components in success. Finding your passion and purpose and sharing it with a partner, co-workers, family or team members will increase the probability of having a happy and successful life.

MONEY

Steve Jobs on facing his mortality stated, "My goal in life isn't to be the richest man in the cemetery." It is important to note this wealthy genius came to this realization "upon facing death" due to terminal pancreatic cancer. As we live day to day, without thought of the finite nature of our life, we often are not as full of such perspective. Most people as they are trying to amass their material fortunes do so at the expense of spending time with their spouse, children, family and friends. *Time, not money, is our most precious commodity. Take time to spend away from work and always be willing to trade money for memories.*

In a speech by Bryan Dyson, former CEO of Coca Cola stated, "Imagine life as a game in which you are juggling five balls in the air. They are Work, Family, Health, Friends and Spirit and you're keeping all of these in the air. You will soon understand that Work is a rubber ball. If you drop it, it will bounce back. But the other four balls-- Family, Health, Friends and Spirit--are made of glass. If you drop one of these; they will be irrevocably scuffed, marked, nicked, damaged or even shattered. They will never be the same. You must understand that!"

Money alone cannot buy a significant life, and will surely not be the sole measure of success. Rather, success can be attributed to helping others, being kind, tending to your friends and loved ones, feeding your mind, body and soul and finding your passion and purpose. When *Kindness* is brought into the picture of *Success*, it will rework the image of what being successful can mean.

PASSION AND PURPOSE

I chose to use both words because they are often used synonymously, but they are very different when it comes to describing choices one makes in *life* and *career* paths. By life, I mean how you live it, who you are as a person and how you treat others. By career paths, I mean what you choose to do for a living and whether or not you made the right choice.

William Shakespeare spoke to this in the most direct words, when he wrote, "The meaning of life is to find your gift. The purpose of life is to give it away."

If we substitute the word "talent" for "gift" in Shakespeare's quote it may be easier to understand. God has given each one of us certain talents at which we can excel.

Talents are usually accompanied by interest and enjoyment. What we focus on in life is a direct determinant of the results we will achieve. If we study 5 hours on our math homework and zero on English, it is highly likely you will get a better grade in math. If you practice the piano 3 hours a day and the clarinet collects dust, you will most likely obtain proficiency in one over the other. People tend to enjoy something they are good at, and consequently usually strive and put effort into getting better. Someone's talents usually indicate a profession where they can have the most *value* and do the most *good.*

I'll repeat what Mark Twain said to open this chapter, "The two greatest days of your life are the day you are born and the day you realize why." For some people that realization of why you were born—what you were made to do--may be music, for others it could be science, others athletics and so on. Someone may have enjoyed geography in high school and did well at it but when school ended so did geography for them. Possibly they didn't think there was any future in it, except maybe teaching. Yet another person may have been a three-sport star and lived and breathed everything sports related, but was told they were never going to be a pro, so their athletic pursuits ended with their last team or season. With that, they relinquish their passion and find that work is something you have to do, but not something you necessarily like to do.

I advise people to be acutely aware if some career direction is tugging at your sleeve. Don't make the mistake of many who were *told,* or they themselves *though*t, a youthful passion was only a passing phase, not something long term where you can turn a childhood joy into a career.

Look at the high school sports champ and see how many career options related in some way to the games he loved as a teen. Coach, scout, athletic director, sports writer or announcer, possibly a sales representative for a sports equipment or apparel company.

The geography fan who thought teaching would be the only career option: how about becoming a tour guide, travel planner, town planner, airline employee, pilot or travel writer. Don't assume there is only one job possibility for your passion.

Following your passion is simply utilizing God given gifts (talents), which intersect with interests to result in a rewarding profession.

Choosing the wrong profession will take you out of character. The wrong career can make you frustrated, envious, angry and depressed by the thought of having to go to *work* another day.

Another frequent discussion I have with my students will illustrate why taking this seriously can be crucial to your happiness. I ask the student what they plan on doing for a career. They tell me they were *thinking* about becoming, for example, an accountant. When I ask why, they usually explain it as a stable field with good pay and that accountants are always in demand. I couldn't argue with that.

I ask what an accountant does and what a typical day would be like. They give me a confused look and finally admit they don't really know and aren't sure what it would be like day in day out. Then I ask why they would be willing to commit forty or more years of their life to something they don't really know much about, not knowing whether they would enjoy it or absolutely despise it.

What if five years into the job they hated it so much they felt they had to do something else? But now they are married and have children and bills and a mortgage. It is too late; you will be stuck because of those responsibilities.

They mull it over and then agree they should spend a little more time planning their future and exploring possibilities. I think it was the part about being stuck in a place with too many responsibilities to make a change that did the trick. That's the timing part I mentioned. As you get older not only does time pass you by, but opportunities to experiment and experience different work directions will pass you by as well.

That is why I tell my sons, and others, "try to do what you *love* to do, before you're *forced* to do what you *have* to do." My direct questions make them aware of a potentially unfulfilling career path, demonstrate the importance of self-awareness and early discovery of appropriate career options. It is best to find a vocation where you experience fulfillment and enjoyment. Money should not be an overriding factor in making such a career plan.

Once you find your passion and purpose, never lose sight of the WHY you chose this path in the first place. Often times stress, work-related conflicts, money and salary issues and office politics will concern you to the extent you fail to focus on the purpose of your work. WHY you chose this avenue-what were the reasons? Helping others, making a contribution to society, a true love of the tasks of the work, etc. We need, especially in times of stress, to revisit that WHY and re-focus our thoughts to the positive. If we no longer can do that, it's time to move on!

The following stories, *A Tale of Two Ways,* are illustrations and examples of finding the better way vs. the hard way to turn your passion into your career.

Before they were married, Jimmy's girlfriend, Chelsea, was a perfect case study of someone who was not starting her career in pursuit of her passion. She received her Bachelor's degree in Sociology, was rejected from Graduate Schools and was looking for *jobs.* Understandably she wasn't very enthusiastic about her future career choices.

We talked about this one evening, and I sensed she wasn't happy with her current prospects. I probed a bit and found that she was considering a number of menial positions and her primary motivator was money since she had bills to pay. This is never a good situation. It's basically desperation. As you know, desperate people often do desperate things, which can send their future speeding down the wrong career path.

Casually, I continued our question and answer session and included some of the pointers we listed earlier: likes, dislikes, things that came easily to her and so on. Then I asked her the *zero* dollar question. If money was not an issue whatsoever, what would she really want to do with her life? In other words what was her passion? Chelsea didn't hesitate. She said wanted to work in the fashion industry more than anything and had for the longest time.

Her sudden enthusiasm indicated a burning desire, a passion in the truest sense of the word. It also convinced me she should work in fashion and, if she took the brave first step, she would succeed. I encouraged her to follow that path and told her she would regret it for the rest of her life if she didn't. I'll admit I also added a message about timing. *"Try to do the thing you want to do before you're forced to do something you have to do."*

Chelsea got the point and found the courage. She took the word *"money"* off the top of her goals list and replaced it with the word *fashion*. She then did her homework on companies to contact, reworked her resume, began to network and get the word out. Not surprisingly, and in relatively a short time, she secured an internship at a local fashion company.

As it turned out, that company did business with larger fashion companies in New York City. She leveraged her experience and new contacts and made it into an entry level job in New York. She also began to attend fashion school while moving around to various entry level positions to gain as much experience and exposure as possible.

She eventually moved to New York City with my son, continued working for a fashion label while simultaneously progressing towards her degree. All of this, despite a sociology degree and many people telling her not to bother with fashion because it wasn't possible with her training, education and background. Imagine if we didn't have that one short conversation and Chelsea wound up working in a *job*. A job which where she had no passionate interest and would face a life riddled with "what ifs."

The second example will show you the hard way, or the long way to arrive at your passion. This longer, more arduous path to get to the point in your life where you are doing what you want to be doing. For that matter, doing what you *should* be doing. It's the path I took.

Unlike Chelsea who was young, only 24, when she got on the right track and began to realize her career dreams, I was 38 when the tug on my sleeve to redirect my life began.

It was more difficult to give up money because it was much needed to raise four children, pay a mortgage and the prospect of high school and college tuition loomed in the future. In many ways, I was the person stuck in his career with no room to move because of the responsibilities of life.

I'm sure for many in similar positions as mine, and the same age as me, the story would end there. The prospect of taking a leap to another way of life was too daunting. Because if they failed, they also failed as a provider for the family. I get that, and at times, almost did the same as them. Nothing. Maintain the status quo.

But the tug on the sleeve didn't stop, in fact it got even stronger. This is where you have to acknowledge that you may not be able to make a leap, but that you can make baby steps to achieving happiness—reaching personal success.

In theory, my plan to do sports camps in the evenings after work and on weekends sounded fairly simple. This meant I was sacrificing most of my leisure time, which was hard on my family life. But this is where my passion began to morph into a job. It also where my family began to become integrated into my passion by helping out at the camps--my boys even registered to attend the camps. It became a family affair.

Of course the income from my Athletic Director job and camps combined still did not stack up to what I was making at law, but the sacrifice of some dollars for my passion was an easy choice. I find that when you are in touch with your passion, positives flow from every direction and you ultimately realize that money cannot buy your happiness.

HEALTH

"If I knew I was going to live this long, I would've taken better care of myself."

Mickey Mantle

My father used the above quote from New York Yankee Mickey Mantle when he was an older man reflecting on his youth. Mickey Mantle, one of the greatest baseball players of all time, wasted his prowess and good health on alcohol and cigarettes and as a result died too young. My father was an avid cigarette smoker throughout his life, and as a young man, he didn't believe that smoking would kill him. This is somewhat understandable, as there wasn't as much information about the side effects of smoking in his time, but it also stems from something more universal that isn't specific to his generation. Young people generally believe they are invincible and immortal, and so they make poor health decisions while they are young without worrying about the consequences later in life.

It's true that you can't prepare for every health emergency, and that sometimes they are out of your control, but you can do your best to avoid them. You can also learn to accept your health and live a productive life in spite of any issues that may occur. It's important to focus on health decisions and habits at an early age.

Well-being consists of physical and mental health, and the two are connected. If you are physically fit, then your mind stays active and your body releases chemicals that make you feel happy. Your mind and your body are extremely important, and although working on one often improves the other, it is necessary to work on them separately.

Daily exercise is important to mind and body health. A solo walk may be a time for you to think about your day and digest the things that are going on in your life, or you may really get enjoyment out of a team sport. It's important to choose something that nourishes your soul as well as moves your body to get the benefits in both areas.

This rule also applies to your diet. A varied and healthy diet, like a varied exercise regimen, is the key to physical health, and perhaps more importantly, the key to enjoying the process of becoming healthy.

In addition to eating the right food, it is crucial to eliminate unhealthy substances from your life. The science is clear: smoking is bad, excessive alcohol consumption causes liver damage, fast food is toxic, and drugs ruin lives! I find that successful people are the ones who avoid these dangers, and as a result, have more energy and wake up feeling good.

Unlike physical exercise, the effects of a healthy mind cannot easily be measured. Overall, a healthy mind allows you to remain positive and see the best in every situation. It eliminates any phrases like, "This is the end of the world" or "My life is over." Instead, with a healthy mind you say, "I will get through this" or "This experience will teach me a useful lesson."

To become more mindful, take a few minutes out of the day and listen to your breathing. Slow down and sit with your thoughts. Learn to appreciate everything that is around you. Be grateful that you are alive. Regular moments of reflection and relaxation recharge the mind, and allow you to see the world clearly and with a sense of awe, wonder and gratitude. As you move through life, you'll find that the main benefit of a healthy mind is that it allows you to cope with unexpected issues that arise. Most important of all, a healthy mind can give you the strength to deal with an unhealthy body, if that becomes your fate.

You cannot always prevent bad things from happening to you. When it comes to life and health, *"you must play it where it lies".* In the game of golf, you always play the ball where it lands. If you hit the ball into the rough, you cannot pretend that you are on the green. You first need to acknowledge that you are in the rough before you get out of it. The same applies to your life and especially your health. You must accept your condition before you can think about getting better, and you must never feel sorry for yourself or let any mental or physical health problems hold you back from achieving your dreams.

There have been countless examples of people that have not let health issues ruin their lives, and my son Casey is one of them. He lost most of his teenage years to drug addiction. During this time, the light at the end of the tunnel often seemed out of reach. I knew that he needed help, but drugs are so destructive, and I honestly wasn't sure we could save him. For a long time, it seemed hopeless.

I doubted myself as a father. I did my best to guide my children in the right direction, and I thought that I did something wrong. I blamed myself for a while, but at some point, it sunk in this was my son's reality, and I realized that so much was out of my control.

If he wanted to get better, the first thing he had to do was accept his condition. Rather than blame himself or go back to an earlier time before this happened, he needed to embrace the present moment and find a way to improve it. As a family, we stepped out of our denial, became less judgmental and more supportive. Instead of lecturing him we educated ourselves on drug addiction in an attempt to understand and this allowed us to be of help.

I learned drug addiction is a complicated disease. On the one hand, those who become addicted make the decision to use drugs, and most of them know that drugs are dangerous. On the other hand, once a person is addicted, it's useless to moralize and say, "You should've known better." Instead, the only option we had was to help our son recover. We all make mistakes in life, and this was my son's mistake. With our guidance and his hard work, eventually he overcame his addiction, and to this day, he remains sober. What's more, he spends his time helping other addicts recover, and I truly believe that his passion to help people today would not have come to him without this difficult experience.

MAKING AND KEEPING FRIENDS

"You can make more friends in two months by becoming interested in other people than you can in two years of trying to get other people interested in you."

Dale Carnegie

Few things in life are as valuable as your friends. They are the ones you laugh and cry with, and the ones who know you better than anyone else. The difference between a happy person and an unhappy person is often enduring friendships.

Remember *"you don't have to be friends with everyone, but you should always be friendly to everyone".* Friendships begin with a simple act of kindness, and you won't make any friends if you aren't nice to people.

At a time when people have hundreds of friends on Facebook, it's important now more than ever to cultivate meaningful friendships. You need to have people that you can talk to rather than text, and that you can see rather than face time. A friend is more than someone who knows your name and says "hello" to you in the hallway at school or in the office at work. A friend is someone who devotes their free time to you and who enjoys your company.

Avoid bad influences and friends that get you into trouble. Don't compromise your morals in order to be liked. If you don't get rid of the people that bring you down, you'll never find the people that lift you up. "Show me your friends and I will show you your future." Never stop evaluating your friendships. If a friend starts dragging you down with their negativity, or if their personality has drastically changed for the worse, or if they become a bad influence, you aren't obligated to remain friends with them. Friendship is a two-way street. You should always be there for your friends, but if you're the one carrying all of the weight, perhaps you need to rethink the relationship. It takes a great deal of bravery to stand up to your enemies, but even more to stand up to your friends.

When we're young, we think that we'll meet many people with whom we'll connect, and so we take our friends for granted. We fall out of touch with people we've known for years and assume that we'll meet a suitable replacement. As we get older, we realize that this rarely happens. Lasting friendships require work and effort on both sides.

There are billions of people in the world, and most of us only form deep connections with a few. I can count my close friends on one hand, and I don't even use all of my fingers. My purpose isn't to frighten you, but to prepare you. The reason why so many people are unhappy in middle age is not because of their jobs, but because they don't have any friends with whom they can share experiences. In order to avoid becoming one of them, make and keep your friends.

It is important to support your friends through tough times. Show up when it counts. Make the effort to see your friends, especially those that don't live close to you. Set a date and commit to it. Try not to cancel. If you do something hurtful, apologize immediately and try to make amends. If your friend does something hurtful and shows remorse, forgive them. Life's too short to throw away your friends, and it's too long if you don't have any.

It's simple to know who your friends are in the beginning. Most friendships begin organically, and you'll naturally gravitate toward those you like. Over time, however, friendships require work and effort to maintain. When all is said and done, lasting and positive friendships will be among your greatest accomplishments.

FAMILY and RELATIONSHIPS

We have now reached, what is in my opinion, the most important element of success, happiness and living a meaningful life. It centers around people and more specifically, your family and relationships. I call this THE RULE OF THIRDS!

I came to a realization many years ago that life can be broken down into a compilation of thousands of days. These days can be broken down even further into what I call my *Theory of Thirds.* Your life can be separated into three 8-hour periods each day. The time you spend at school or work, the time you spend with loved ones like friends, family, or a significant other and the time you spend asleep.

The *First Third*, which consists of the time you spend at school or work, is the one people seem to focus on the most. They spend most of their time, money, and energy on endless educational courses, vocational research and training, standardized tests, meetings with counselors, etc., only to come to a decision as to what school they should attend or what career path they should choose. These decisions become the primary focus, which is unfortunate because your school or career path can always be altered or changed, and, as previously noted, should constantly be revaluated throughout your life in search of your *Passion and Purpose.*

If you are unhappy with your school choice, especially college, you can transfer. If you hate your job, you can seek different employment or make a career change, all with some discomfort but nothing too life altering. The *First Third* is flexible, but the *Second Third* is less, and as a result, it becomes the most important.

The *Second Third* consists of the time you spend with friends, family and most importantly, the person with whom you may decide to share the rest of your life. The consequences of a bad decision in the Second Third can be the most damaging of all. Toxic friends or an unhappy home life are more harmful than a poor career choice, and the negative impact is often permanent. It is easier to change a job you dislike and you may soon get over it, but it is not as easy to get out of a painful marriage or rid yourself of those destructive friends. You can't always make up for your mistakes in your personal life. Your boss will most likely give you a second chance if you make a mistake at work, but your spouse or best friend may not. Unlike the *First Third*, the grief associated with the *Second Third* is not short lived, and poor decisions can stay with you for the rest of your life.

With so much at stake, why don't we put as much time, effort and resources into the right choice of a partner or friend? As we concentrate on obtaining the best degree and a career that can provide us with all of life's comforts, we fail to realize the importance of choosing the right partner with whom we will settle down, or the right group of friends with whom we will spend our free time.

In my own life, I have had multiple career changes and have easily survived after short periods of discomfort. By contrast, I have been divorced just once and can say with certainty the turmoil caused by that event was far greater in magnitude than any school or career change I have made. I was fortunate to have my oldest son, Jimmy, from my first marriage, but the stress involved in the prospect of not being there for him every day was overwhelming and lead me to physical illness and destructive life choices. While I spent plenty of time and energy on my career, I did not think nearly long enough about the decision to marry my first wife. In retrospect, I should have focused more on the *Second Third* and less on that *First Third*.

After my divorce, I met my present wife, Kim, who accepted my son Jimmy as her own. She encouraged me to stop making destructive personal choices. She supported me in every career move I have made, and has blessed me with three other sons and a tremendous family life. Now I know that the right choice in the *Second Third* allowed me to have a successful *First Third*, whereas a wrong choice in the *Second Third* when I was younger resulted in unhappiness that made the rest of my life unbearable.

The *Final Third*, sleep, is also significant, and I have found that it works out well when I make the right decision in my relationships. When my home life is happy, I always sleep well. During short periods of upheaval in my professional life I have had some sleepless nights, but they paled in comparison to the sleepless nights caused by stress in my personal life. We all know the feeling of being unable to concentrate at work or school and not sleeping while being constantly preoccupied with relationship problems.

Therefore, my best advice is to take as much, if not more, time choosing the people with whom you will spend that *Second Third* of your life. If you do this, the *First Third* will work itself out when the right people are by your side and you will also sleep better!

Remember money, careers, prestige and even your health will have little meaning unless you have the right people to share them with.

Lesson to Remember

Set proper priorities in your life. Find a life filled with passion and purpose. Always make your health and friends and family a focus and, try to find the right person to share your dreams and goals with.

Personal Assessment

Are you scrutinizing your relationships as much as you do your proposed career paths? Do you know what your passion might be? Is it in sync with what you do or want to do for a living?

Changing the World Challenge

Do some self-evaluation:

- List the things you love to do and/ or enjoy the most.

- What skills do you have?

- What things do you excel at?

- What comes easily to you?

- List the people you admire and what they do. Are there any similarities among them?

- Recall and examine your early childhood. What did you like to do most then?

Study your findings. A pattern and a passion profile should begin to form. Do your passions align with your career? Is there a way for you to better incorporate your passions into your daily life? How can you create more time to be with family and friends and ways to improve your health all of which will ensure personal success?

Jim and his wife, Kim

Jim with his best friends

*Jim Coaching
Future Stars*

*Jim as assistant coach of the McDonald's
All American Game in Indianapolis*

*Jim with friend and
legendary NBA'er
Manute Bol*

Mr. James Olayos
Director of Athletics

Jim as Athletic Director

Recognition Award from the United States Military

No matter what happens in life,
be good to people.
Being good to people is a
wonderful legacy to leave behind.

Taylor Swift

LEGACY

How do you want to be remembered in the Mall?

For the vast majority of us, we can only hope our legacy will be akin to a *ripple*, a gentle flow, spanning generations and positively impacting our family, friends and even strangers we might never directly encounter.

While the legacy, good or bad, of politicians, celebrities and modern day "influencers" may be immediately visible, they will never intimately touch the souls of our beloved ones and those yet to come.

Emerson said, "it is one of the most beautiful compensations of life, that no man can sincerely try to help another without helping himself."

I hope as you have read this book you have come away with certain definable thoughts on how you wish to be remembered and the impact you can have on this world. My desire is to help you find a life that feels good on the inside, not one that always looks good on the outside.

I can illustrate this goal by sharing a simple realization I had after spending time with my family in the mall. My long involvement with sports, education and kids programs in general has allowed me to make many friends and even more acquaintances. When my wife and boys would walk through the mall with me, it was inevitable I would cross paths with someone I knew. We would exchange hellos and simple conversation and then move on to our next stop. Every time that person would walk away one of my children would ask me, "Who was that?" I knew they were not interested in a long dissertation on the details of our relationship so I would give them a quick thumbnail sketch on the person they just met. I would say "high school teammate, great guy," sparing them details on his prowess as a player etc. Sometimes I would respond, "that guy has an important job, but not a good person." No reason to go further on that one! Other times "classmate in college, they treated everyone nice."

Then one day came my realization that hundreds of people were walking away from **ME** and were being faced with the same question. What would they say about me? I made a vow that day and reaffirmed what I already thought, I would try hard to live my life in a way that my legacy and reputation were that of simply a *"Good guy"*. I asked myself, *"how do you want to be remembered in the mall?"*

Hopefully I would be remembered as a person who valued his family, friends and his most important relationships, to feel I lived epitomizing one my son Jimmy's other tattoos *"Family First"*. A person who acted in kindness and walked in faith with a sense of respect for others at the forefront of all my actions. A person who represented, both by his words and actions, a life of integrity worthy of the desire of others to follow my lead. To set an example, to those I have met along the way, on how placing kindness at the forefront created, for me, a life much richer than you could imagine.

The aforementioned wish for a far reaching and impactful legacy is simplified by a very humble personal wish. I believe it is best reflected by the following story.

When I was 8 years old my mother started a scrapbook for me. She filled it with my sports accomplishments, newspaper articles, report cards and other items of memorabilia. On page one she placed the following prayer, written in 1950, as reminder to me of the Legacy her and my father wished for me. It was not a prayer for athletic fame or fortune or great riches, it was an ideal and a wish that still sits on page one of the scrapbook today. This prayer is so meaningful to me it was placed on my son Jimmy's funeral card, as he was the epitome of the following words.

A GAME GUY'S PRAYER

DEAR GOD:

Help me to be a sport in this little game of life. I don't ask for any place in the lineup; play me where you need me. I only ask for the stuff to give you a hundred percent of what I've got. If all the hard drives come my way, I thank you for the compliment. Help me to remember that you won't let anything come that you and I together can't handle and help me to take the bad breaks as part of the game--help make me thankful for them. And, God, help me always to play on the square, no matter what the other players do. Help me to always come clean and help me to see that often the best part of the game is helping the other guy. Help me to be a regular fellow with the other players.

Finally, God, if fate seems to uppercut me with both hands and I'm laid up on the shelf in sickness or old age, help me to take that as part of the game also. Help me not to whimper or squeal that the game was a frame-up or that I had a raw deal. When in the dusk I get the final bell, I ask for no lying complimentary stones. I'd only like to know that you feel I've been a Good Guy.

Chaplain's Digest

What better legacy can I have than to have followed in my grandfathers, fathers, uncles, coaches and mentors footsteps? What better legacy than to be thought of as **"A Good Guy"**. Their legacy continues to *ripple* through me while I hope my legacy will flow through my sons, my players and those that have met me.

What will your legacy be when you get older? Will your legacy create a positive *ripple* effect for future generations?

A Game Guy's Prayer

"Oh God

"Help me to be a sport in this little game of life. I don't ask for any place in the line-up; play me where you need me. I only ask for the stuff to give You a hundred per cent of what I've got. If all the hard drives come my way, I thank You for the compliment. Help me to remember You won't let anything come that You and I together can't handle. And help me to take the bad breaks as part of the game. Help to make me thankful for them.

"And God, help me always to play on the square, no matter what the other players do. Help me to come clean. Help me to see that often the best part of the game is helping the other guys. Help me to be a regular fellow with the other players.

Finally, God, if fate seems to uppercut me with both hands, and I'm laid up on the shelf in sickness, or old age, help me to take that as part of the game also. Help me not to whimper or squeal that the game was a frame-up, or that I had a raw deal. When in the dust I get the final bell, I ask for no lying complimentary stones. I'd simply like to know that You feel I've been a good guy."

A Game Guy's Prayer

Biography

Jim Olayos was born into a family where kindness ruled. As he grew, Jim absorbed his childhood experiences and focused on developing his own character—to become the kind of man who would make his parents proud. As an adult, Jim studied kindness—and the many traits that fall under the umbrella of kindness—through his work in a school setting. This led him to formulate a thoughtful way of self-conduct that inspires and educates those around him, especially the youth of New England.

Jim has touched more than 20,0000 children since he founded The Future Stars Sports Academy and Children's Foundation in 1997. Part of the Academy's instruction is *Lessons of Life*, a unique character-building program that instructs children on the fundamentals of being a good person. Sadly, those basic and important elements of respect, responsibility, kindness and honesty are no longer emphasized in many homes and schools.

Over the years, many national and local organizations have recognized Jim's efforts in the sports world and for his work with children. *USA Today* bestowed its "Most Caring Coach" Award on Jim and the *New York Daily News* named him "Coach of the Year." *World Kindness USA* has recently recruited Jim as a National Board Member for Athletics. He earned the Sportsman Award of the Greater Bridgeport Athletic Association, was voted one of the 100 Most Influential People in Connecticut High School Sports, and was honored by The YMCA of Connecticut with its "Distinguished Service Award." The *New York Times* has also featured the *Lessons of Life* program and Jim's sports academy and foundation.